The Skin Between Us

The Skin
Between Us

A Memoir of
Race, Beauty, and Belonging

KYM RAGUSA

W. W. Norton & Company
NEW YORK · LONDON

For information about permission to reproduce selections from this book,
write to Permissions, W. W. Norton & Company, Inc., 500 Fifth Avenue,
New York, NY 10110

Manufacturing by RR Donnelley, Harrisonburg
Book design by Brooke Koven
Production manager: Andrew Marasia

Library of Congress Cataloging-in-Publication Data
Ragusa, Kym.
The skin between us : a memoir of race, beauty, and belonging / Kym
Ragusa.— 1st ed.
    p. cm
ISBN-13: 978-0-393-05890-1 (hardcover)
ISBN-10: 0-393-05890-5 (hardcover)
1. Ragusa, Kym—Childhood and youth. 2. Racially mixed people—New York
(State)—New York—Biography. 3. Grandmothers—New York (State)—New
York—Biography. 4. Feminine beauty (Aesthetics)—Social aspects—New York
(State)—New York. 5. African Americans—New York (State)—New York. 6.
Italin Americans—New York (State)—New York. 7. Harlem (New York,
N.Y.)—Race relations. 8. New York (N.Y)—Race relations. 9. Harlem (New
York, N.Y.)—Biography. 10. New York (N.Y.)—Biography.   I. Title.
    F128.9.A1R345 2006
    974.7'10040551096073092—dc22   2005033673

W. W. Norton & Company, Inc.
500 Fifth Avenue, New York, N.Y. 10110
www.wwnorton.com

W. W. Norton & Company Ltd.
Castle House, 75/76 Wells Street, London W1T 3QT

1 2 3 4 5 6 7 8 9 0

for
Vivek Bald and Edvige Giunta
and
in memory of my grandmothers

Acknowledgments

This book is a subjective look back at certain events in my life and in the lives of my family. I have woven a narrative out of many bits and pieces: fragments of my own memory; family stories passed down through the generations and altered in the process with each telling; interviews with family members; snippets of adult conversation I overheard as a child. It is my own interpretation of events as I have experienced, understood, and remembered them. Undoubtedly others represented in the book will have their own interpretations. To that end, I have changed the names of many of the people I have written about, in order to protect their privacy.

Portions of this book have appeared in earlier forms in the following publications: *tutteStorie* 8: "Origini—Le Scrittrici Italo Americane" (Maria Rosa Cutrufelli, ed. 2001); *The Milk of Almonds: Italian American Women Writers on Food and Culture* (Louise DeSalvo and Edvige Giunta, eds. The Feminist Press, 2002); *Are Italians White? How Race Is Made in America* (Jennifer Guglielmo and Salvatore Salerno, eds. Routledge, 2003); *Leggendaria* 46–47: "Italiane

7

D'America" (Anna Maria Crispino, ed. 2004). I am deeply grateful to the editors of these publications for supporting my work in its many stages and for introducing it to a dynamic, critical, and encouraging audience, both in the United States and in Italy.

I thank my editor at W. W. Norton & Company, Alane Salierno Mason, for believing, from the beginning, in the importance of my story, for giving me the opportunity to tell it on a larger scale, for helping me to give it shape and nuance, and for having the patience to allow it to come in its own time and on its own terms. In many ways, it was she who called this story into being. I thank my agent, Geri Thoma, for her great faith in the book when it was just an idea, for helping me to see and to reach its potential, for her gentle guidance and her fierce support, for her humor, her clarity, her personal integrity and strength. She is a constant inspiration to me.

I also thank Alane Mason's assistant, Vanessa Levine-Smith, for her great generosity, kindness, and patience in guiding me through the production process. I thank Geri Thoma's assistant, Julia Kenney, for her enthusiastic reading of my manuscript at its earliest stage.

I have been blessed with many mentors, brilliant and uncompromising women, writers, and readers, who believed in me without question and who pushed me to write, think, dream, and be in ways I never imagined possible. I thank my English teachers at the Convent of the Sacred Heart, Victoria Taylor, Eileen Brady, and Suzanne Price, for encouraging me to live a life in books. I thank Hettie Jones, in whose memoir workshop at the 92nd Street Y I began to write this book, and whose early enthusiasm for my story gave me the courage to keep writing. I thank Joyce Johnson, whose memoir workshop at the 92nd Street Y and the smaller group that evolved from it provided a space for me to struggle through the tough lessons of voice and craft. She pushed me, through her teaching and through the example of her own work, to write with simplicity, precision, and grace. I also thank my fellow writers in each of these workshops for their support, their criticism, and their comradeship, especially Chaya Deitsch and Corinna Barsan. I thank Jan Clausen, friend, colleague, and mentor, for her faith and encouragement through all the years when I was circling around the writing of this book, not knowing yet that I would write it. She showed me, through her own art and life, that the personal can be deeply, truly political. Finally I thank Louise DeSalvo. She was there at the birth of this book; her practical guidance, her emotional support, and her creative advice made it possible for me to write and publish my story, and to begin to live my life as a writer. I am honored now to be in her MFA class in the Creative Writing program at Hunter College. Her talent, courage, generosity, honesty, and humility astound and inspire me daily.

There have been so many people who have influenced and inspired me in the making of this book, and I want to thank specifically those who have been there from before the book was even an idea, whose love, friendship, conversation, and creative example have been beacons of light in my work and in my life. There are four people whose spirits pervade this book, and whose friendship over the years has given my life shape, meaning, and much pleasure: I thank Lyle Ashton Harris, Susannah Ludwig, Jennifer Guglielmo, and Jyoti Mistry. I also thank Lina Pallotta, Mauro Magrini, Kim Masterson, Patricia Eva Oppenheimer, Phyllis Capello, Rosette Capotorto and Ronnie Mae Painter, Mike Poppleton, Florian Schattauer, Sangeetha Kamat and Biju Matthew, Jocelyn Luckett, Joseph Sciorra, Sunil Bald and Yolande Daniels, and Richard Fulco. With so little space there are many people I cannot include by name, and I extend my sincere thanks to them. I trust they know who they are and how much I appreciate their friendship and support.

Many thanks to my dear friends and colleagues: Catarina Romeo for her beautiful and sensitive translations of my writing; Mary Gannett of BookCourt for her heartfelt and inspiriting early reading of the manuscript; and Hiram Perez for his generous and creative criticism and contextualization of my work.

It has been my great fortune to be part of two communities in which I have grown tremendously as a writer and as a person. In their embrace I have felt the pleasures of belonging and have developed some of the most important relationships of my life: the Malia Creative Collective and the Brooklyn Writer's Space. I also thank Stefano Albertini and New York University's Casa Italiana Zerilli-Marimo for providing a nurturing and welcoming home for my own work and that of my Malia sorelli.

I thank Thrae Harris for her compassion, her wisdom, and her invaluable presence in my life. I thank John Edgar Wideman for his encouragement and his kinship, and for telling the world the story of Sybela Owens and the beginning of Homewood.

I thank my mother and father for giving me the best of themselves. I thank my *ma*, Suresht Renjen Bald, whose love and support mean more to me than I can say.

This book is dedicated to my husband and best friend Vivek Renjen Bald. His brilliance, goodness, and integrity are boundless. His faith in me and his belief in the necessity of my story have been unshakable from the beginning, and I have learned to be a better writer, a more honest writer, through his fierce criticism and spirited praise. I thank him for teaching me, again and again, the meaning of the word "home."

This book is also dedicated to Edvige Guinta, sister of my heart, writing partner and cumma'. Her tireless and profound work as a critic, scholar, teacher, poet, and memoirist literally opened the way for me and for a larger community of Italian American women writers and artists to do our work and to share it with ever-growing audiences, readers, and supporters. It is through her work, and her love, that I finally found my way back to my history, my community, and my voice. I thank her for showing me the way to be whole.

This book would not have been possible without them.

Contents

13

The Skin Between Us

Prologue

I stood on the deck of a ferry crossing the Strait of Messina, the narrow tongue of water that separates mainland Italy from Sicily. It was an early morning in the beginning of May. The sun had just risen, and the sky was a soft Easter-egg blue which seemed to bleed at the horizon into the deeper blue of the water. It was cool for that time of year, with a bite in the air. Nothing like what I had expected. I was unprepared for this journey, as I often have been. I pulled my thin sweater up against my throat to keep warm as the salty air rushed past. The water was calm but for the ferry's wake, creamy white-tipped waves radiating out from either side of the prow as the boat heaved forward. And all around a strange absence of sound, nothing but the deep rumbling of the engine. I couldn't hear anything else, no lapping water, no cries of seabirds, no laughter from the other passengers who stood in clusters around the deck. I gripped the rails tightly and closed my eyes, a little seasick from staring too long into the swirling water below. For a moment I lost myself in the dizziness, in the engine's roar and its vibrations beneath my feet.

Behind me lay Calabria, the toe of the Italian boot. Just ahead—

so close that I could imagine reaching out and touching it—was the northeastern shore of Sicily. Long ago—the dates are unclear and those family members who could remember the details are long dead—my paternal grandfather's family migrated from Sicily to Calabria. By the beginning of the twentieth century most of the family had left Calabria for New York. But I have another connection to this part of the world: Sicily is the crossroads between Europe and Africa, the continent from which my maternal ancestors were stolen and brought to slavery in Maryland, West Virginia, and North Carolina. Two sets of migrations, one forced, one barely voluntary. Two homelands left far behind. Two bloodlines meeting in me. A common joke among Italian Americans is that the toe of Calabria is kicking Sicily back to Africa, where it really belongs. If you see it on a map, it really does look that way. As the ferry drew closer, I could make out villages clustered around green hills, barely visible behind thick strands of slowly passing clouds. Just ninety miles beyond was the coastline of Tunisia.

The ferry wasn't very full this time of day, this time of year. I looked around me at the other passengers who had come out from the enclosed seating area aboveboard: a middle-aged couple leaning into the bracing air, holding hands, and a group of men standing together drinking espresso in little paper cups from the concession stand. I thought they must all be Sicilians, some returning to the island for a short visit, some going home after work or vacation in other parts of Italy. Every now and then someone threw a furtive, disapproving glance my way. What must I have looked like to them? A woman alone, already an oddity. Already suspect. My dark, corkscrew hair was pulled back, something I had learned to do whenever I went someplace where I didn't want to stand out, which for most of my life had been most of the time. I had that feeling, all too familiar, of wanting to climb out of my skin, to be invisible. My skin, dark or light, depending on who's looking. *What are you?* people have asked me for as long as I can remember. In Italy, people ask me, *Di dove sei?* Where are you from? I thought about going back inside the waiting area. Despite the chill, I could feel drops of sweat gather behind my knees.

It was 1999. A little over a year before, both of my grandmothers had died of cancer, one week apart from each other, my paternal grandmother Gilda following my maternal grandmother Miriam to the other side like an immigrant crossing the ocean to meet her sister in a new country. Since then I had lived in a state of numb devastation, stumbling through the days as though I had lost my own eyes. Miriam and Gilda had been the unwavering magnetic forces of the two poles that had defined my life. Miriam and my African American family, Gilda and my Italian American family. The neighborhoods where they had each lived in Harlem a few avenues away from each other, yet worlds apart. The neighborhoods they had each left in search of someplace better, someplace safer. I had spent most of my childhood and young adulthood traveling between their homes, trying and not always succeeding to negotiate the distance—cultural, historical, linguistic—between them. Now they were gone, but my life was still cleaved in half. I didn't know how to stop shuttling, back and forth, back and forth, and now there was no one on either side to meet me, to show me that the journey was worth it. Would always be worth it.

What home was I searching for that chilly May morning on my way to Sicily? Soon we would be landing in Messina. I would have a long trip ahead of me that I didn't know if I had the courage to make. Death had propelled me there, an ocean away from Harlem. But it was Harlem I was thinking of, longing for, just as Miriam and Gilda had longed for it after leaving it so long ago. I had to come this far to know that I needed to find my own way back.

CHAPTER ONE

I only have one photograph of myself with my two grandmothers. The picture was taken on Thanksgiving in 1996. In another year, they would both be gone. But here in the photograph, in the alchemy of chemistry and light, they are alive, they are glowing, together. That Thanksgiving we all had dinner at Gilda's house in New Jersey. My husband had rented a car and had driven Miriam, my father, his girlfriend, and me out early that morning, the trunk filled with bags of groceries for the meal. My mother stayed home that day, as on most holidays; she was never enamored of family gatherings and the unspoken emotions they always threatened to exhume. Gilda was alone when we pulled into the driveway, waiting as she always did at the porch door, waving from behind the glass. My cousin Marie and her husband, who lived in the apartment upstairs, were with his family at the Shore. At one time I had also lived in that house on Boyden Avenue, with Gilda, my father and stepmother, my grandfather Luigi, Marie, and her mother, my Aunt Angela. My grandfather and aunt had died years before, and the family unraveled. My father didn't visit very often from his home in Manhattan. Gravity seemed to be pulling Marie and me into our adult lives, and Gilda toward the end of hers. Looking back, though, I see that Miriam's rare presence here gave me the illusion that this gathering was a beginning, not an ending.

In the three decades of my life, Miriam and Gilda had been together under one roof, sharing a meal, only a handful of times. Somehow, through the years, they had grown close, if you could call it that. In spite of the distance, or maybe because of it. I was the sole connection between them, the conduit through which they found a way to talk to each other, to respect each other, to turn to each other for comfort, especially in those last years when they were both ill. Often they communicated through me, sending messages and love to each other back and forth between my visits. But this year was different. They were sitting together at the kitchen table, holding hands and laughing at a joke I couldn't hear. I watched them from the island counter as I chopped carrots, onions, garlic. My father stood at the stove, frying sweet Italian sausages for the stuffing, wiping his brow with a worn kitchen towel. My Indian-Scottish-Australian-American husband, Vivek, washed salad greens at the deep enamel sink and Susan, my father's Russian-Jewish girlfriend, pulled the leaves off branches of rosemary and thyme, filling the kitchen with a kind of ancient forest smell. An American Thanksgiving, to be sure. I can still see the blur of Susan's pale, freckled hands and hear my grandmothers' laughter, rising into the air and mingling with the elemental aromas of cooking and baking. How could I know then that all I would have left of that day were the memories made, recorded, and held within my senses? The photograph is the only proof I have that it really happened, that it was not something I merely wished for, a dream of wholeness that could revoke all the separations, all the silences and anger that filled so much of our lives together.

The picture is of the three of us sitting at the dining room table after dinner, Gilda to the left, Miriam next to her in the center, me a little off to the right. None of us look at the camera—I don't remember who took the picture, although I suspect, because it seems such a candid moment, that it must have been my husband, a filmmaker, always looking to capture his subject off guard. Those are the most honest moments, he says, although I see another kind of honesty in the pose of the portrait, something always flickering behind the composure of the sitter, some fleeting thought, some unconscious emotion pushing its way through to the surface. Here, in this unstaged image, there is also so much under the surface, so much that can't be expressed. All that the three of us struggled through to get to this point.

Gilda is glancing sideways out of the frame, her eyes are lowered, her face almost grave. No sign of her earlier laughter. By this time much of her mind had given way to Alzheimer's disease, the beginnings of which appeared long before her cancer. Her thoughts were clear sometimes; mostly she spoke haltingly, trying to remember the names for common things around the house, or what year it was. Trying to sort the living from the dead, who equally made appearances in the jumble of her memory. What could she be thinking here? She's wearing her sleeveless blue cotton housedress, the one she always wears, no matter what the weather. The one that brings out her sapphire eyes, the same as my father's, and shows off her thick worker's arms, now fleshy and dimpled. Her face is deeply lined, her white hair is floating in wisps in the light falling on us from the lamp hanging above.

Most of the light is on Miriam. It shines on her red hair, straight and fine as Gilda's, pulled back into a ponytail held with a red velvet ribbon. Her hair was always ornamented in some way, with great silver barrettes or silk flowers or wide straw hats with feathers in their brims. She's dressed in purple—her favorite color—a sweatshirt and matching pants that she somehow makes look chic. Her oversized glasses with the rosy frames make her look so smart and familiar, like a favorite librarian in a small-town library, who always knows just the right books to suggest. Miriam's smile is broad and generous, embracing everything around her. There is no sign of the pain she's in, of the spreading cancer; she looks strong, as she always has, as I've always needed her to be. At sixty-four, she's a full generation younger than Gilda. But death, when it comes, will not make such a distinction. I'm struck by the quality of Miriam's gaze, turned toward Gilda, even as Gilda looks away. It's the look of a hard-won love, of quiet victory. It took years of struggle, this tender gaze. It was work.

I'm at the other end of the table, my face half in the light, half in shadow. My hair is pulled back—even here, at home in many ways, I'm hiding. I smile shyly, my chin resting on my hand. Watching my two grandmothers together, amazed. Eternal daughter, made of their mingled flesh and blood. Their lives extended through mine. I look so much like both of them: Gilda gave me her sharp nose and small build, and Miriam gave me her smile and her upturned eyes.

On the table there is a big salad bowl, our empty salad plates still in front of us. In Gilda's house, as in Italy, each course of a meal was served on a different plate, and salad came after the main dishes. In Miriam's house, all the courses were enjoyed together on the same oversized plate, her thick, sweet Russian dressing, bright orange, mixing with all the other flavors. At Gilda's the salad was made with oil and vinegar, salt, a little oregano. The bitter tastes here, the sweet tastes there, my palate formed by them both. We are only halfway done with Thanksgiving dinner. There will be fruit and roasted chestnuts, cannoli and coffee after the table is cleared. The bottle of wine will stay, though, sipped through to the end of the evening. Our glasses are empty, a moment of peace between the three of us, truce. The window behind us frames us, the night outside is thick and black. We are like a still life, the objects on the table, the angle and warmth of the light. The three of us suspended in time, a study in composition. How did we get here, sitting together, sharing a meal? Two warring communities, two angry and suspicious families, two women tugging at my heart, pulling me in different directions.

We have almost the same color skin. Our skin is the truth that this image has captured. Gilda's thin, wrinkled skin like paper left out in the sun, Miriam's plump, barely lined, mine always a mark of difference, even here, even though it's not all that different. Three variations on ivory, yellow, olive, refracted between us like a kaleidoscope. The skin between us: a border, a map, a blank page. History and biology. The skin between us that kept us apart, and sheltered us against the hurt we inflicted on each other. The skin between us: membrane, veil, mirror. A shared skin. There were storms behind us and there would be darkness ahead of us, but in the photograph all that is held at bay. We are held together for a moment by a warm light and a kitchen table, and everything makes sense.

What are you?
Black and Italian. African American, Italian American. American.

Other. Biracial, Interracial. Mixed-blood, Half-Breed, High-Yellow, Redbone, Mulatta. Nigger, Dago, Guinea.

Where are you from?

. . .

I DON'T KNOW where I was conceived, but I was made in Harlem. Its topography is mapped on my body: the borderlines between neighborhoods marked by streets that were forbidden to cross, the borderlines enforced by fear and anger, and transgressed by desire. The streets crossing east to west, north to south, like the web of veins beneath my skin.

IN MIRIAM's kitchen in Harlem, there was a little clock radio. Miriam always kept it on AM, mostly news. I liked to turn the tuner back and forth, looking for songs I knew and singing along. There was a song that was popular at the time that I used to think someone wrote about my parents. Whenever it came on, I turned up the volume, sat up close to the little mono speaker. It was about a white man and a black woman who were in love. The man in the song had my father's name. The woman was nameless, invisible except for her blackness, or because of it. I understood that this was a sad song, that the man and the woman couldn't be together because he got into a fight with his parents when he brought her home to dinner. Somehow I understood that this must have happened to my mother and father, even though I wouldn't hear the stories about their courtship until much later. Whenever the song came on, I imagined them finding their way back to each other, loving each other still. I imagined that one day, as in a fairy tale, they'd run away together, and take me with them.

My parents met at Columbia University in 1964. They weren't students, no one in their immediate families had ever gone to college. My mother was a secretary in the admissions office; my father was a clerk in accounting. They worked in the same building, passing each other in the halls, riding the elevator together, surrounded by other clerical and service workers, professors and students, stealing glances at each other. My mother was seventeen years old. I have a photograph of her from that time, a simple black and white headshot, maybe from her high school yearbook. Her hair is straightened into a *That Girl* flip, bangs partially hiding her dark almond eyes. She's wearing a neat Peter Pan collar; around her neck is a tiny gold cross. She will always wear a cross around her neck. She has just graduated from parochial school; her life is all possibility, all expectation. Each day she walks up the hill on 110th Street, along the tattered northern edge of Central Park, past the crumbling tenement buildings that gradually give way to fraternities and faculty housing with doormen. Her expression is open, blank, revealing nothing of the person she might have been then, the person she would become. But she was beautiful, exotic in the white, upper-class world in which she and my father found themselves and each other. My father had never seen anything like her.

My father was twenty. His whole world had been the few blocks of his Bronx neighborhood, a predominantly Italian world. Before his job at Columbia, he used to work in a deli not far from his house. He'd learned to make every kind of sandwich, learned to slice mortadella and capicola, provolone and Swiss cheese, thin and supple as summer leaves. It was a good trade, something to stick with. My grandmother Gilda would say to him, *Learn the business, maybe open a little place of your own someday.* But my father was beginning to get curious about the world beyond the neighborhood. So he quit the deli job and found work in Manhattan. Every morning he took the number 6 train from Westchester Square back to East Harlem, where he had been born, when that neighborhood was still referred to as Italian Harlem. He walked up 116th Street, through El Barrio, through black Harlem, up to Columbia's pristine campus. On his days off he explored. His older brother Tony lent him jazz records, took him to see Coltrane and Miles play down in the Village. A photograph of my father around this time shows him sly-eyed and goateed, playing a set of bongos, almost a cartoon image of a beatnik.

One day in the elevator my mother handed my father a piece of paper. It said, *Ti voglio bene.* She told him that someone had said these words to her, and asked him what they meant. *I love you,* he told her. My mother had thought him handsome and had asked around about him. When she found out that he was Italian, she was intrigued. He was as exotic to her as she was to him. So they began to see each other. In secret, most of the time. Interracial marriage was still illegal in some states. Even in New York City, neighborhoods, schools, and social scenes were still resolutely seg-regated. When my parents walked together in Harlem, black men would sometimes threaten my father, and yell at my mother, *"What's the matter, you too good for a black man?"* When they walked together downtown, white men would spit at them; once some-one called my mother a dirty gorilla. Women in both parts of town shook their heads at them in disgust. My parents went to movies and cafés in the Village, where things were a little more relaxed, but my mother was no bohemian. She had ambition, wanted to be something, anything. Wanted most of all, desperately, to get out of Harlem.

SHE TOOK MY father to meet Miriam. They all sat in the living room, my mother and father next to each other on the orange plastic-covered couch, Miriam in a chair across from them. Miriam had made coffee and her special chocolate cake with the extra-thick frosting—this was an occasion, after all. She hadn't known what to expect when my mother first told her she was dating a white man. Face to face with my father, she could barely hide her disappointment. She believed, as many other black people did, that Italian Americans were nothing but mafiosi, racists, and republicans. If my mother was going to aim for a white man, why not something better? My father was barely white. Sitting in this room in Harlem with Miriam and my mother, in fact, he was the darkest one there. For the rest of the afternoon, the three of them sat in painful silence, my mother trying to make small talk, my father complimenting Miriam on the cake one time too many. A slow-burning anger began to rise from the pit of Miriam's belly, sticking in her throat. She had dreams for my mother. Hoped one day she'd go to college, become a doctor or a lawyer. She saw my father taking it all away, getting my mother pregnant and leaving her after his particular case of jungle fever subsided. Finally, Miriam got up and told my father to leave, told him that he couldn't see my mother again. *You're not going to ruin my only daughter,* she called out behind him as she shut the door. *You're nothing but poor white trash!*

He took my mother to meet his parents in the Bronx. When they walked into his building, people standing outside stopped what they were doing and stared at her. My father took her hand, right in front of them. Gilda and Luigi were certainly not expecting him to bring home a black woman—my father had only told them that my mother was different, not Italian, which was bad enough. They were in shock when they saw her. Still, Gilda served Italian pastries and espresso as they sat around the old mahogany table in the cramped dining room. My mother watched my father and his parents stir spoonful after spoonful of sugar into their coffee, and did the same, nearly choking on the dark, syrupy thickness. Luigi said a few polite words in English to my mother that she couldn't understand because of his heavy accent. Gilda avoided conversation altogether, hurrying from the table to the kitchen and back again, busying herself with cleaning, preparing the dinner. My mother would not be invited.

The next day Gilda would cry to my father, *Why, why? Che vergona!* The whole neighborhood knew by now that my father brought a nigger, a *moulignan'*, into his house. Brought shame on his parents. Gilda stopped talking to my father, serving him his meals in silence for a week. Luigi was philosophical. His son was an American, after all, and a man. Let him have a little fun. But if my father's sister ever brought a black man home, he would kill her.

SOON MY MOTHER was pregnant. Abortion was illegal; my mother knew the stories about girls who died trying to throw away babies by themselves, drinking Drāno, tearing up their insides with wire hangers. She hid the pregnancy as long as she could. When she started to show, she got fired from her job. My father began putting extra money under his mattress, a few dollars a week. A huge silence hung over them both. Meanwhile, I floated in another kind of silence, growing blood and bone inside my mother's womb. A mingling of bloodlines, a mutation of genetic codes. Their bodies fused forever in my becoming.

I was born in late afternoon at the end of February 1966, in the teeth of winter. New York still had real winter then, blizzards, punishing winds, frozen sidewalks. As a kid you might wake up in the morning, rush to your window, and see nothing but a field of white. You'd pray for a snow day, turn on the radio, and listen to the announcer go through the list of schools that would be closed, the public schools first, then the private. When the name of your school came on you'd dance back to your bed in your footy pajamas and pull the covers over your head. I like to think that I was born on a snow day, when all the kids in New York City were home, one big play day when the usual rules did not apply.

My mother says she gave birth to me alone. She was in a hospital on the Upper East Side, a teenage black girl, an unwed mother. She doesn't remember much about the days just before and after I was born, how she got to Lenox Hill, why she didn't end up in the old Women's Hospital in Harlem, so much closer to where she lived. Alone in the fancy maternity ward, ribbons of pain snapped at her body, and the white nurses in their white polyester uniforms handled her without tenderness. My mother says my father abandoned her while she was pregnant. My father says he wanted to marry her but she refused and didn't want to see him anymore. The truth has floated somewhere between them all these years, fragile and unspoken, permeable as one of those bubbles I used to blow with the little plastic wand. The bubbles used to hover, prismatic in the air, just out of reach. If I tried to grab one, it would pop, sticky and soapy in my palm.

MIRIAM WAS SILENT when I asked her where she was the day I was born. She said only, *Your mother knew she always had a home with me.*

SO MY BIRTH was not met with the usual fanfare, the proud father with the cigar, the relatives streaming into the hospital room, showering the mother with kisses and congratulations. My mother went home by herself the next day, the snow gathering in swirls around her as she held me. She never told me how she got back to the apartment in Harlem. Did she hail a cab by herself on the street in front of the hospital? Did a girlfriend pick her up and drive her home? A crib was set up for me next to her bed in what would later become my room. I don't know who called to tell my father I was born, or when.

Two artifacts exist from the time of my birth: a photograph and my birth certificate. The photograph was taken when I was a few weeks old. I'm propped against a pillow on a nubby green couch, my head lolling a little to one side. I have thick dark hair and a red face; my eyes are puffy and squinted. I don't know where this picture was taken—it wasn't Miriam's apartment—or who took it. There's no one else on the couch; I'm alone, adrift on its wide green sea. I wonder if my mother was waiting for me, somewhere outside the frame. My birth certificate has a line for my mother's name and her age, eighteen. The line for my father's name has been left blank. Officially my father does not exist. He has escaped responsibility for my mother and me, at least on paper. When my parents were born, birth certificates still had a category for race. In some ways, things have changed: there is no line for race after my name. For the moment, at least on paper, I have escaped classification.

CHAPTER TWO

My earliest memories of the apartment in Harlem are of the sound of women's voices, my mother's and Miriam's the most familiar, sometimes mingled with the gravelly voices of my elderly great-aunts, who would visit from Pittsburgh a few times a year: a constant flow through the days and nights, of whispers and laughter, arguments and lullabies. There was another voice, early on; I must have been around two years old, maybe even younger. I strain to recognize it now, the memory of another woman singing to me in a voice unlike anyone else's I knew. I remember that I couldn't quite understand the words to her songs, but even now I can call back the feeling of falling into the embrace of her words. She called me baby. And she fed me honey. A line from my childhood I will never forget: *A spoonful of honey each day will keep the doctor away.* She would say this, holding a small spoon to my mouth, and I would take in the sweet stickiness, hold it under my tongue, hold it for as long as I could and then let it slip down my throat.

Her name is lost to me. All I know about her is that she was a woman from the Caribbean Miriam had hired to help take care of me when I was still in diapers, while she and my mother worked the many jobs they held in those years. How do I speak of this without shame? Shame at the long history of black women's bodies and labor used in the service of white women and their children, of slave-owning freedpeople and their privileged descendants. And here was Miriam, a light-skinned black woman living in a black community, employing a darker-skinned woman to watch over me. Who held her children while she held me? I imagine Miriam coming home from work in the evening, taking me from this woman's arms—did I cry at that moment, passing between two sets of maternal hands, one dark, one light? Miriam gives her money for the day's work—how much could it have been? The woman puts on her coat, maybe pats me on the head goodbye. Where does she go when she leaves here? Will she send her wages in a letter to the island she comes from, to the woman who is caring for her own children? I began my life within the shadow of a past that is impossible to escape. But this woman, from another corner of the diaspora, planted a seed in me. She put honey on my tongue, and there, slowly, words grew.

Even at two, three, four years old, race, and its contradictions, were embedded in my most innocent thoughts and desires. Someone had given me a music box—I don't remember who, or for what occasion. I have a clear image of myself holding it. It was made of wood, painted white with fake gold trim, something that you'd get at the five-and-ten. When I opened the box it played a few bars of a song that was popular at the time, the notes high and tinkling, wavering a little. The inside of the box was covered with red velvet, and there was a tiny plastic ballerina on a platform who turned around and around. She wore a white tutu and a gold crown. Her skin was pink and she had bright yellow hair. On the inside of the lid was a mirror, and I could see myself in its reflection, could see my own brown eyes peering in as the dancer twirled in front of me. I would open and close that box, the music stopping and starting, so I could peek in to see the ballerina rise up as the lid opened. I loved that moment, how she rose and turned.

I began to dream of being a ballerina one day, dancing on my tippy-toes and wearing a skirt that floated up when I moved. I remember then wanting pink skin and yellow hair. This was what all ballerinas looked like, wasn't it? And if I wanted to be a ballerina, I would have to have the same pink skin, the same yellow hair when I grew up. There was nothing in my consciousness at this point to tell me this wasn't possible. After all, Miriam's skin was almost pink and her hair was red. I must have imagined that whiteness was something I'd just grow into, like when you got your grown-up teeth. I wonder now how I held all those incongruities at bay: my love for the dark-skinned woman who cared for me, the differences in skin color, hair texture, and physical features between Miriam, my mother, and myself, the sparkling, oblivious blond world outside our home and neighborhood that I was only just beginning to perceive.

What was constant was women and their work. The bustle of household activity inside our apartment: my mother bathing me in the kitchen sink, Miriam stirring pots on the stove, the steam moistening strands of hair so they stuck to her forehead, Aunt Gladys on her hands and knees scrubbing the hallway floor. And the work they did outside that I would never see. My mother carrying plates lined along her arms in restaurants, feigning delight as a male customer slaps her miniskirted ass. Miriam typing letters in the office of a campaigning politician or picketing in front of City Hall against the latest budget cuts, those that would affect Harlem, as usual, in the worst ways. As I got older, I would begin to understand how the reality of women's labor permeated our whole building. Women in the other apartments working their day jobs in factories and shops, or, if they were unemployed or on welfare, mopping the stairs, washing the walls in the downstairs entryway, scrubbing graffiti off the metal door of the elevator. A whole underground economy based on what women could do to get by, and to help each other. One woman set up a hair salon in her apartment, traded washings and settings for home-cooked meals. Others watched each others' children, or ran errands for women who were ill or too old to make it up and down the steps when the elevator was broken.

The women in the building literally kept it functioning; I remember meetings Miriam would host in our apartment to strategize about what the tenants needed to do to take the landlord to court when the boiler broke down yet again, when weeks would go by without heat or hot water. Pots of coffee in white pitchers sat on the table, and someone would bring sugar cookies or a plate of Ritz crackers with a brick of cheddar cheese. As a small child I would sit on the floor in a corner and listen, sneak over to the table to take whatever sweet I could reach when I thought no one was looking. Here was my mother's friend Jackie from the second floor, slipping in after putting her baby to bed. Here was elderly Miss Sally who lived one flight above us, who would lower grocery money in a basket tied to a rope to her grandson as he played in front of the building. *Don't get any candy,* she'd call down to him from her window, *and bring back my change!* Here was Mattie, an enormously overweight young woman who lived alone on the ground floor, lowering her fleshy hips into a chair. I would stare at her swollen feet, barely covered by slippers with slits down the middle to accommodate them. I couldn't understand what Miriam and the other women were talking about, but I recognized the anger and the tired frustration in their voices. When I was a little older I would help them make signs that they would put in all the street-facing windows during rent strikes. I'd write *No Heat, No Rent* with a thick Magic Marker in my best, neatest handwriting, always checking with Miriam that I spelled all the words right. The women would leave the meetings late in the evening, stretching, gathering up purses and notebooks, arms around each other's shoulders.

I have no memory of my mother at these meetings. She's always said that she has no interest in politics, though I've never quite believed her. *Nothing ever changes,* she says with a shrug. She must have watched Miriam all those nights, cleaning up the paper plates and coffee cups after the neighbors had gone home, then putting the percolator back on the stove, sitting down at the kitchen table to draft letters to the landlord, the housing board, the city council. In my imagination, my mother comes into the kitchen, pours her mother a fresh cup of coffee, watches her write. They're both bundled in coats and sweaters to keep out the cold air rushing through the gaps in the windowpanes. Maybe next week the heat will be turned back on, though it will surely be cut off again. The hot water will disappear, and my mother and Miriam, like all the other women in the building, will have to boil water in huge pots on the stove so we can bathe. Or someone's space heater—the cheapest one is all most people can afford—will short out and set their apartment on fire. I remember being torn out of bed late one night, being held by my mother as she climbed out of our fifth-floor window onto the rusty fire escape, staring down at the fire trucks in the street below. Miriam is behind us with Dorothy, her Siamese cat, in her arms. Fire is pouring through the building, and our apartment is filled with black smoke gushing past us through the window. It feels like I'm swallowing mouthfuls of steel wool, even as I gulp down the icy winter air. The sound of shrieking sirens is everywhere. On the sidewalk, I can see some of our neighbors who live on the lower floors. They're covered with blankets, pointing up and crying. I can never remember how we got down that rickety fire escape, whether a fireman reached out to us from his ladder and brought us to safety. For a long time after, I believed this fire—actually there were more than one of that magnitude over the years—was a product of my imagination, a story I made up somewhere in childhood. But my mother assures me that it was true, and now when I think back to that time, I can see the scorched wall that led to the door of our apartment. In all the years that we lived there, it was never repainted.

My mother's response to all this had always been private—she kept her fear, or her anger, or her shame, to herself. Instead she would escape, by immersing herself in a book, or going alone to the movies. Sometimes she'd take me with her—we'd go from one theater to another, munching on popcorn and hot dogs, sometimes seeing three or four movies in a day. My favorite theater was somewhere on the East Side—we'd have to take a crosstown bus and then a downtown bus to get there. The walls of the lobby were painted with trees of every height and shade of green. It was like entering an enchanted forest. Whenever we got there early, we'd sit at one of the little wrought-iron garden tables near the concession stand. My mother would get a soda for herself and a chocolate egg cream for me, and I would run my fingers along the painted leaves, wondering what they smelled like and what birds lived among the branches. The first film that I remember seeing—I was around four years old—was *Cabaret*. It has always been my favorite film, and I like to think that I first saw it in this theater. It's difficult now to understand what I saw in this grown-up story set in Nazi Germany. But something about the exuberance of the singing and dancing, the tilted bowler hats and velvet shorts with red hearts at the crotches, and Liza Minnelli's sleek black hair and green fingernail polish, grabbed hold of my imagination. When the curtains closed and the lights came on, I begged my mother to stay so we could watch it all over again. We must have seen it ten times in a couple of months. We'd leave the theater singing, *Life is a cabaret, old chum,* all the way back to the uptown bus stop.

Often my mother would take a bus by herself down Fifth Avenue to look in the windows of fancy department stores. She would spend hours wandering from Bendel's to Bergdorf Goodman to Saks, gazing at the latest fashions displayed on impossibly tall, thin, blue-eyed mannequins. She'd watch rich women come out of the revolving doors, their arms loaded with shopping bags, teetering on high heels to the curb, where they waved their jeweled hands at taxis. My mother would tell herself that she deserved what was in those bags, just as much as anybody else. When she came back home she would describe to me the wonders in those store windows, the sheer silk minidresses in psychedelic patterns, and suede jumpsuits dyed brilliant red, and floor-length white mink coats. *One day I'll have a coat just like that,* she'd say.

MIRIAM AND MY mother had moved into our apartment in the early 1950s. Miriam had been living in Los Angeles with her husband, an actor. The marriage had been unhappy from the start, and there came a point when she couldn't take it anymore. She had written to her Uncle Sheldon, who lived in Harlem, asking him to help find a place for her and her small daughter. He wrote back saying he knew of an apartment on 111th Street and Seventh Avenue, just across from the north end of Central Park. A friend was moving out that month. She'd have to take it right away. Miriam never spoke about how it felt to make the decision to leave everything and start a new life across the country, all in a matter of weeks. She had dreamed of living in Harlem for as long as she could remember—if she had any doubts about making it on her own, any second thoughts about ending her marriage, she kept them to herself. She got on a Greyhound bus with my mother, who would have been around six years old, carrying only a couple of suitcases and all the money she had, hidden in a hat box. A few days later they arrived in Harlem.

Miriam would always tell me how proud she was to live in our building. *A real prewar, just like the apartments on Park Avenue. Stately,* she called it. I didn't notice its hidden grandeur when I was growing up. What I saw, each day, was a limestone exterior blackened by decades of air pollution, a dark, narrow concrete front courtyard which led out to the sidewalk where I was never allowed to go by myself, the cornice missing from the roof on one side of the building, as if it had been blown off during a war. I couldn't appreciate the parquet floors of the lobby, or the huge marble staircase that spiraled up the center of the building. I saw only the missing stairs, sometimes replaced with rotting plywood, sometimes not replaced at all, so you always had to watch where you stepped, in case you fell through. But this is my adult memory speaking, looking back from a distance, my vision narrowed by grown-up resentment. Would I have judged the building so harshly as a child, or would it have simply been home? I wonder how my mother felt looking up at it for the first time as a little girl holding Miriam's hand, if the building would have been safer, cleaner, less neglected than it was when I was growing up. Their house in L.A. with the large backyard, so close to the ocean, was gone forever. My mother would only see her father a few more times, and then he, too, would disappear. She's always said that she doesn't remember anything from that time, that she was too young. But from the day my mother arrived in Harlem, whenever anyone asked her where she was from, she would always say, *California.*

I try to picture their first few months in Harlem. My mother adjusting silently to a new school, catching up quickly. Her awkward first attempts at new friendships. I imagine her learning the route from home to school, memorizing the order of the streets and avenues, which way was downtown, which way uptown. Miriam searching for work and meeting her neighbors—what must they have thought of each other, Miriam looking like a white lady with her little honey-colored daughter, the women in the building welcoming but guarded, so unlike her privileged friends back in L.A. Miriam must have been shocked by the disparities between her old life and her new home, and between Harlem and the rest of New York. She discovered that the best—and closest—grocery store was up the hill near Columbia University, where shops and restaurants of every kind catered to the needs and desires of moneyed white people. Many of the shops near her own apartment had closed down in the wake of the riots of the 1940s and the subsequent flight of the black middle class—even in the early 1970s, I remember only a candy store, a liquor store, and a laundromat, all partitioned by bulletproof glass.

Miriam would also have discovered how isolated Harlem could be from the rest of the city. From the beginning, she and my mother were afraid of the subway. After years of living in a place where the ground could literally open up and swallow you whole, they weren't going to take any chances with the crumbling subway system. Bus service was limited between Harlem and other parts of the city—you had to walk for blocks just to find a stop, and then often wait a half hour or more for the bus to arrive. Just a few years after she arrived, Miriam would join a boycott with hundreds of her neighbors against the MTA, demanding that more bus lines be directed through Harlem.

Sometimes on weekends Miriam would take me with her on

one of her shopping expeditions to the discount stores on East 86th Street. We'd accumulate bags full of stuff: marked-down toiletries and cleaning supplies, thin dish towels and floral-motif plastic teacups made to resemble fine English china, pantyhose for Miriam, a pretty nightgown for my mother, cotton underpants and undershirts for me—all "slightly irregular." We would go from store to store for what seemed an eternity, with Miriam searching out the best bargains. I was always getting lost in the ladies' lingerie department, fascinated by the garter belts that looked like sea creatures with flapping tentacles and huge "DDD" brassieres that I thought were made for giants. Miriam would inevitably find me and pull me sulking along behind her. But she'd always give me a reward at the end of the day, an ice-cream cone or maybe a cross-eyed baby doll she'd find in the discontinued bin. If she felt like she had found some really good deals, Miriam would splurge and we'd take a taxi back home. Suddenly she'd put on a strange face, her chin held high like she was searching the sky for some invisible star. She'd say to the white driver in a quasi-British accent, *1809 Seventh Ahvenue, please. Okay, lady,* the driver would say, and we would be off, flying up Park Avenue with its impassive face of blond apartment buildings, their shiny windows empty as eyes.

These uptown rides hadn't always been that easy. Before she started using the accent, soon after she'd arrived in New York, Miriam would struggle with her shopping bags into the backseat of a taxi, give the address, and the driver would refuse her. *I don't go that far,* he'd invariably say, and tell her to get out of his car. At some point she realized she could increase the bargaining power of her light skin by speaking like some wealthy society matron and acting as if she lived at one of the most coveted addresses in all of Manhattan. Oddly enough, this charade usually worked. The driver would crane his head around to get a good look at Miriam, think she was white, and decide he was going someplace safe. There were still times, though, when no driver would take her, even when she had me with her. They would tell her to get out, and start to speed away before she had finished getting me and all her things out of the backseat. Sometimes the bags tumbled out, spilling their contents into the gutter. I'd watch her bend down to collect the debris as other cabs drove past us in a yellow blur, and I'd try to help, running after an apple rolling down the sidewalk, pulling a new scarf out of a puddle. Once we collected everything, Miriam would take my hand and turn away from the curb—back straight and nose in the air—and figure out another way to get home.

I THINK THE excitement of living in New York must have tempered those early disappointments, bolstered in both Miriam and my mother a sense of possibility that they would always carry with them. *The greatest city in the world,* Miriam always said. In their first few months here, she would take my mother to the Empire State Building, Radio City Music Hall, Grand Central Station. They would walk together for hours, always looking up, at the tops of buildings—gleaming, arched, patrolled by gargoyles, modernist flat. They'd wander down the deep canyons of Wall Street and the financial district, take a ferry to the Statue of Liberty. I see the two of them in each of these places, snapshots that were never taken. Hope and determination mingle in Miriam's eyes—a new, barely imagined phase of her life is unfolding before her. In my mother's eyes there is still innocence, and something else—acquiescence?

If there was a moment when she might have forgiven Miriam for taking her away from her father and California, from everything she knew and loved, it would have been one like this: They're up on the observation deck of the Empire State Building, taking turns looking out across the city in one of those funny viewfinders that look like surprised cartoon faces. My mother, standing on the tips of her toes, can see buildings and streets and parks, the Hudson River glinting in the sun. Miriam guides the viewfinder to face north. *See the end of the park?* she says to my mother. *That's where we live. That's home.* My mother looks out at the cotton-candy tops of the trees, tries to make out the building on 111th Street. From this distance, it's all one swirling, breathing mass of silvers and greens underneath the bright blue sky, like a child's finger painting.

It was the world beyond the park that Miriam would grow to love best. Harlem both frustrated and exceeded the youthful fantasy she had once held of living there. She would not find men in top hats and women in fur coats and endless good times. That had been her mother Mae's Harlem, and even then it had been only a partial truth. Miriam did find many kinds of good times: the nightclubs where the great jazz musicians of the era—Miles Davis, Dizzy Gillespie, and Thelonious Monk among them—could be found playing on any night of the week. The block parties on Saturday afternoons where women sold slices of homemade cherry pie and elderly couples danced in the blocked-off streets until the sun went down. The long walks arm-in-arm with her girlfriends along the wide, tree-lined avenues on Miriam's days off, eating ice-cream cones they got for ten cents at the soda fountain after window-shopping. But the Harlem of the 1950s was also a place of growing popular unrest, of picket lines and boycotts and increasing activism among ordinary black people: apartment building tenants, schoolteachers, men who had come back home from the front lines of World War II and found that their heroism abroad hadn't translated into jobs and equal rights back home. These became Miriam's neighbors, her friends, her lovers. All of it made Harlem what it was, and all of it made Miriam fall in love with what she would always call "the Black Mecca."

Uncle Sheldon would sometimes take Miriam to parties so she could meet people, maybe find a boyfriend or a future husband. She loved going *out on the town,* especially to the rent parties that were held on Friday nights all over Harlem. Sometimes she would help friends plan theirs; she'd decorate their living rooms with colored streamers and drape lace cloth over the lampshades, and she'd make big bowls of punch and platters of macaroni salad. She seemed to be most comfortable in the middle of things, organizing, directing, moving the furniture. Only far into the evening would she relax, stop refilling people's drinks and sweeping the cigarette butts off of kitchen floors. If the right song came on, something by Nat King Cole or the Platters, she'd allow herself to be led to the dance floor by a suitor, allow herself to get lost in the darkness and the swaying and sweating of the bodies around her. In later years, she would put her energy into political work, where the field of action was so much larger, and where she could feel herself to be part of the daily making of history. She would describe to me the visits to Harlem of Kwame Nkrumah, Fidel Castro, Nikita Khrushchev, how she would be one among thousands of people crowding the streets to greet them. She seemed to be always where the action was, but behind the scenes, in the background.

The apartment on 111th Street became another canvas on which Miriam could express her desire to organize people, events, and the space around her. The layout of the apartment was unusual: a bedroom and living room on one end of a long, narrow hallway, a larger bedroom and a small bathroom and kitchen on the other. A third bedroom was oddly placed in the middle of the hallway, and seemed miles away from whatever was going on in the rooms at either end. The front rooms—the living room and Miriam's bedroom—were shut off from the rest of the apartment by French doors. I was not allowed to pass through them uninvited. I knew that this was where life happened. Where Miriam served her guests rich dinners of pig's feet and sauerkraut or the dreaded chitlins, which filled the house for days on end with a deathly pungency, and homemade desserts that she prepared at dawn before she went to work and stored in the Frigidaire for later. The grown-up women of the house—Miriam, my mother, Aunt Gladys, and the other Pittsburgh relatives whenever they visited—gathered here after their long days, sipping mugs of Sanka with their feet up. It was where the adults talked in hushed tones and watched the news on the big television in its wooden console, images of the war, of demonstrations, of rioting in cities all across the country. Things I wasn't supposed to see.

The front rooms were filled with *things*. On the kidney-shaped wooden coffee table and countless side tables stood lamps with shades of different sizes and colors and specimens from Miriam's small jungle of houseplants, some real, some a waxy plastic; I could never tell the difference. All over the living room there were souvenirs from her various travels, conch shells from Haiti or Trinidad, Mexican vases painted bright pink and blue. Miriam's bedroom was hidden from the living room by a chartreuse brocade curtain, a mystery always just beyond my reach. This room held Miriam's secret life, whatever that may have been in the imagination of a child of my age. I would stand quietly by the curtain sometimes, watching Miriam dress, watching as she pulled on the purple pantyhose that she wore when she was going out at night, worked her heavy, ivory-colored breasts into her brassiere, reached her fleshy arms behind her back to hook it together. I'd inch into the room when she wasn't looking, run my hands along the dresser opposite the bed, picking up whatever I could reach: photographs, a hand mirror, a bottle of 4711 perfume with an atomizer that I would pump in my small hand, spraying the room with its bracing, lemony, masculine scent, until finally Miriam shooed me out.

Every few months, Miriam would throw a big party at home: a fundraiser, a victory party for a new city councilman, a birthday celebration. She would get huge deliveries of Chinese or Indian food, set up a buffet on one side of the living room. She'd buy jugs of red wine and bottles of Cold Duck and six-packs of beer that she would put on ice in the bathtub. On the coffee table she'd arrange platters of crackers with onion dip that she made from a container of sour cream and a packet of onion soup, and pungent Limburger cheese with thin slices of pumpernickel bread. I'd follow her around the house as she cleaned, help her carry things from the kitchen up to the living room. After a while, Miriam would tire of me being underfoot, and I'd have to get ready for bed. I always wanted to stay up, to sit with the grown-ups in their secret world, but Miriam wouldn't hear of it. Just as the party was about to start, she'd come to tuck me in and turn off the light. She would always leave the door open a crack because I was afraid of the dark, and when her guests arrived I could hear her greeting them, her laughing voice like water falling.

I'd sit up in bed, straining to hear everything as the party went on down the hall, ebbs and swells of conversation, glasses clinking, Al Green on the stereo. One time—maybe I was six or seven—I slipped out of my room and tiptoed down the hall, padding giddily toward the music and laughter. The French doors were thrown open and the living room was filled with a lazy red light. The music was loud, the room filled with a sweet menthol haze from the men's Kools and the women's perfume, scent of politics and desire. Miriam was sitting on the long orange couch that hulked against one wall of the living room like a ship at anchor. It was covered with shiny plastic to keep it clean and would stick to bare legs and backs, leaving smears of sweat along its surface, especially when there was a party, with the heat of so much skin and mingled breath.

I must have crawled over the other people sitting with Miriam, my nightgown rumpling up over my underpants. Miriam pulled me roughly into her lap, and I remember the tight look on her face that should have warned me that I was in trouble. I stared at all the ladies with their miniskirts and dangly earrings, the men with their dark suits. How the men and women held their glasses, dragged slowly on their cigarettes, moved in close to talk to each other. How many different shades of brown skin there were in that room, and different accents: Southern, New York, Spanish, West Indian. Somehow I wriggled away from Miriam and ran out into the center of the room—I had decided that I would entertain her guests.

Here I am in the sea of brown legs, shouting at the top of my lungs: *I want to sing a song!* Well, *go on, little girl,* one of the adults calls back, and someone turns down the music. I put my hands on my hips, switch my skinny behind back and forth, and sing:

> *strut Miss Lizzie*
> *Lizzie, Lizzie*
> *strut Miss Lizzie*
> *all night long*

People clap and laugh. I imagine I'm a big star, think they'll ask me to sing another song. But Miriam snatches me up, her face red and her brown eyes flashing in horror. Everyone goes back to what they were doing before. *That's enough!* Miriam whispers to me, dragging me out of the room. *Just wait until tomorrow!*

I had no idea why she was so upset. At that age, I didn't understand that the song I sang to her friends was about a streetwalker, didn't know that the way I was moving my body had something to do with sex. It was just a song that I had learned from some of the older girls in the building, something we'd sing jumping double

Dutch out in the front courtyard. My body still remembers the motions that went with the song, the shimmying and the swaying, and I'm amazed how completely intertwined innocence and bawdiness must have been for me and the other girls I knew. *Shake it to the east / shake it to the west / shake it to the one that you like the best,* we'd shout, swinging our hips and laughing. *It must be jelly, 'cause jam sure don't shake like that.*

It was around this time when I noticed that it felt good when I squeezed my thighs together. The first time it happened I was alone at the kitchen table doing my homework, practicing my spelling and penmanship. It was early summer, during one of those New York heat waves when people really do fry eggs on the sidewalks, just to see if it's possible. I remember the steady scratching of my pencil on the paper and the clammy feeling of sweat at the back of my neck. I could feel the heavy, stagnant air on my legs as they dangled from my chair, and I lifted my skirt to fan myself. In that moment, as the hot air gave way to the light breeze I was making, I felt an awareness between my legs, an urgency, that I hadn't known before. I squeezed my legs together and suddenly I felt even warmer *down there.* I got a little shivery, tried it again, squeezing and letting go, squeezing and letting go. Later I learned to lie on the bed on my stomach, put my pillow between my legs, and rub against it. Even though I didn't understand that what I was doing was sexual, I had a feeling that I shouldn't be doing it, that I shouldn't tell anybody, and shouldn't get caught. But I didn't stop.

After the party, Miriam told me that little girls who act like they're grown get in trouble, that I was a pretty little girl and I couldn't sing and dance like that with men around. "Pretty" sounded like a bad word. What made me pretty, and what could I do to make it go away? All at once, I became afraid that I wasn't safe anywhere. Outside there were people Miriam called "sex-fiends" and junkies who would kill you for a dollar if you left the courtyard. And now at home I had to be afraid of men who were Miriam's friends, afraid of dancing, afraid of my own body, that ultimately it would betray me. This lesson would get reinforced again and again—I was somehow too visible. I had to rein myself in, keep my head down.

We girls were learning a new language in that courtyard, protected on three sides by the gray walls of our building and various mothers and grandmothers who would peek their heads out the window to make sure we were there. But the courtyard was also open to the street, and I remember sometimes men would stop and watch us while we played, until they were hissed away by one of the grownup women coming in or out of the building. We were learning the language of the black female body, of its joys and desires, and also its vulnerability. Miriam, like mothers all over Harlem, tried to keep us alive against the odds that were never in their favor. They tried to cut a path through the chaos for us, tried to make us see clearly the dangers all around us. Teenagers turning to prostitution to survive, toddlers molested by drunken uncles, girls who were raped and then thrown off rooftops. The girls with ebony skin, and cinnamon skin, and sepia skin, the girls with stiff pigtails and sleek cornrows, the girls with shy smiles and the sassy ones who rolled their eyes, the skinny girls and the ones who grew curves before the others, each one precious, each one dreamed for, worked for, cried over.

CHAPTER THREE

Once a year, Miriam's maternal aunts would come from Pittsburgh to stay with us. Aunt Gladys, Aunt Hazel, and Aunt Virginia would descend upon our apartment like great powdered birds, carrying huge suitcases that smelled of mothballs. When Miriam first moved to Harlem, her three aunts had come right away to help her settle in and to look after my mother while she found a job. Later, they helped take care of me. Weeks before they'd arrive, Miriam would turn the apartment upside down, waxing all the floors, vacuuming the curtains in the guest room, plumping new throw pillows against the couch and chairs. We'd go down to the Port Authority bus terminal to pick them up, Miriam pulling me along tightly by the hand so we didn't get separated. One by one they'd appear through the gate, and rush over to Miriam, crying, *Our baby, oh, our baby!* I would stand back shyly as they embraced Miriam, all of them with tears in their eyes, until one of them scooped me up and covered me with wet kisses that left coral-colored lipstick marks all over my face.

At home, they fluttered around Miriam, told her how lovely she looked and what wonderful things she had done with the apartment, the same compliments each year. I never saw Miriam as happy as she was with them. She really did become like a girl in their company, beaming when they praised her. We'd sit together in the living room, and I'd watch the aunts take off their shoes and rub their stockinged toes. Miriam would set before them plates of cucumber and cream cheese sandwiches, and after they ate she'd bring out bags full of gifts for them, and they'd exclaim over her extravagance for hours.

I was always a little afraid of the Pittsburgh aunts. They were black women from another era, and their habits and expressions seemed strange and old-fashioned. And they each had blond hair and light eyes, which made them look unreal, like they had stepped off the pages of a fairy-tale book. There was a sense of cronelike magic and superstition around them—they seemed ancient to me, although when I was a child they must have only been in their fifties and sixties. All three were afraid of Miriam's cat—they believed that cats climbed up onto your face at night and suffocated you while you were sleeping. In the late afternoons, they would sit around the kitchen table quoting Nostradamus and the Book of Revelation, sipping coffee from Miriam's bright orange mugs, balls of fire in their hands. I would try not to listen as they warned that we were in the last days, that the world would soon end and Jesus would judge our souls. The aunts spoke of Jesus as though he were an angry father, and we were all bad children who needed to be punished. This seemed to bring them comfort, but it terrified me. Whenever they'd begin to shake their heads knowingly and say, *It won't be long, now,* I would cover up my ears and yell, *No, no, no,* until they realized that they were frightening me. One or the other would raise a wrinkled finger to her lips, and they'd turn to another subject, the fickleness of the weather or the price of pork chops at the A&P.

Aunt Virginia was the oldest; she had gentle eyes and deeply furrowed skin. I don't know what happened to her husband, he was never mentioned; his whereabouts didn't seem like a deep silence, a terrible secret, but more something that didn't matter enough to deserve to be spoken about. She had a large mole on her chin with fine hairs growing out of it, and whenever she would reach for me, *Come on and give me some sugar,* I would cringe and squirm away. Aunt Virginia had narcolepsy—she called it *the sleeping sickness.* She would fall asleep, just for a few minutes, in the middle of a sentence, snoring lightly, her head tilted back against her chair. A minute later she'd wake up and giggle a little. *Oh, did I fall asleep again? Don't pay me no mind.* And then she'd continue where she left off in her story, an intrigue about a no-good nephew or the latest news about her granddaughter—her great pride— who was putting herself through nursing school. Sometimes she would fall asleep walking down the street and someone would pull her away from an oncoming car. Then she'd wake with a start, thank the person, and go on her way, to the grocery store, the check-cashing place. Aunt Virginia believed that the sleeping sickness had made her psychic—she had forseen the deaths of some of our relatives in Pittsburgh. Since then, she had grown afraid of her own dreams.

Aunt Gladys stayed with us most often, and became like another grandmother to me. She had been widowed early and never remarried. She rarely spoke of her husband, but when she did she would smile and raise her face upward, as if she saw his spirit floating just underneath the ceiling. She smoked a pack of Virginia Slims every day and had a deep, froglike voice that telephone operators would mistake for a man's. *I'm a woman,* she'd scream into the receiver after being called "Sir," and we'd all fall out laughing. Sometimes, when a song she liked came on the radio, she'd do this little dance, raising her skirt and slip a little above her knees, snapping her fingers, and kicking her feet from side to side like Rumpelstiltzkin with soul.

Aunt Hazel was the youngest of the sisters, only ten years older than Miriam. She was very thin—*Your Aunt Hazel eats like a bird,* she'd say to me at mealtime as she picked at her food, always referring to herself in the third person. She wore pastel double-knit pantsuits with printed chiffon scarves tied jauntily at her neck, each day, it seemed, a different outfit, a different color. I never saw her in a skirt. Her hair felt like the softest cotton—she wore it in a kind of pageboy style, flipped up at the ends. She had a tough giant of a husband and two growing sons back home, and I've always wondered how such a delicate woman could live in a house full of big, hungry men. But she was pretty tough herself. When one of her sons, who sometimes came with her to visit us, would get out of line, she would shake her small fist in his face and threaten, *If you don't quit right now, I'm gonna snatch you bald-headed!* The kids on her block back in Pittsburgh called her "that white lady." If she heard them she would yell back at them, *I ain't no white lady!*

I loved these women, though like any child I took them for granted, complained that the house was too crowded when they were around. I was jealous of the adult time they shared with Miriam, of their late-night card games and cackling laughter that I could hear from my room down the hall. And although I wouldn't have been able to articulate it then, their blondness and their light eyes confused me. They were so different-looking from the other people in our building, and sometimes I would catch neighbors throwing them suspicious looks behind their backs. I struggled with the awareness of how different we all were—the three blond aunts, Miriam, my mother, and me—with our eclectic combinations of features, the different ways that the African and the European blended and blurred in our bodies. I remember that I spent a lot of time looking at myself in the mirror whenever the aunts were around—I think I was trying to find some reason behind our difference, some map of resemblance, some sign that it was okay that we looked the way we did.

My own body was a mystery to me when I was growing up—in many ways it still is. My skin is fawn-colored, with yellow and olive undertones. I'm pale most of the time, although in cold weather my cheeks, ears, and the tip of my nose turn a bright red. My knees and elbows are ashy, just like most of the other little black girls I knew in Harlem—Miriam used to rub them with Vaseline. My nose is broad from the front but long and pointy in profile. For Miriam, my nose was a source of pride—she called it my "Roman nose."

I have eyes that turn up at the corners, wide cheekbones, a sharp chin and jawline—my face is all lines and angles, never any baby fat, no softness. *You're lucky you have such fine features,* Aunt Gladys used to tell me. I didn't understand why I should be proud of this. *Fine features are important to have,* Miriam would add, *they'll help you when you grow up.* She never elaborated on what kind of help or why I would need help in the first place. But in the tangle of stories that Miriam and the aunts would tell, I began to learn that "fine" equaled pretty, smart, special.

Once I had barely escaped a fight with Nicole, an older girl who lived on the third floor, whose skin was a deep brown. We got into an argument over something stupid, like who was first in line at the Mr. Softee truck, and she started to push me, shouting, *Bitch, you think you're white.* The other kids started to shout, *Fight, fight,* and I ran back into the building, slamming the lobby door against their rising laughter. For the rest of the time that we lived in the building, I avoided Nicole—I was afraid of her, and ashamed of my fear. I didn't know how to be tough, to stand up for myself, and I blamed this on the color of my skin. My lightness made me weak. At the same time, I couldn't understand Nicole's fury at me, its velocity. Neither of us had a name for the thing that separated us. But I was beginning to see myself as wrong, that something about me could make other people angry. I would need to hide to protect myself, to be invisible so that I didn't offend. I would have to learn how to make myself harmless, nonthreatening, small.

And then there was the matter of my hair. It's the color of roasted chestnuts and curls into tight corkscrews that spring up from my head like tiny arrows. It's kinky in the back, the place the Pittsburgh aunts called "the kitchen," and hardly ever seems to grow there. My hair is not "good," even though my nose is "fine," and when I was a child, this was both bewildering and shameful. My mother and Miriam struggled to take care of my hair, to tame its unruliness by keeping it in tight pigtails. Miriam railed against my father, whose hair is also tightly curled, for ruining mine, for tainting it, those damned Sicilians with their African blood.

Aunt Gladys was the one who dealt with my hair most of the time. Hair was always done in the kitchen—my mother would heat her hot comb on the stove, and Miriam would touch up her gray hairs, leaning over the sink, rinsing the dye out of her hair with plastic-gloved hands. There would always be other activity happening at the same time: Miriam rushing to get dinner ready on a weeknight, Aunt Gladys making a pot of sweet iced tea, my mother on the phone with a girlfriend, painting her nails, and me sitting next to her, blowing on them to help them dry. Our kitchen was a small space, painted a sunshine yellow with a single window that faced the back wall of another apartment building, and looked out onto the inner courtyard below. There were spaces like this behind buildings all over Harlem—I imagine that once tenants sat in their shade in the summer, had picnics or birthday parties for their children, hung laundry together there. But by the time I was growing up in the 1970s the space behind our building was a field of rubble, covered with piles of bricks and broken glass. Miriam had hung the window overlooking the back with bright yellow-flowered curtains, filled its narrow sill with plants.

Once a week, Aunt Gladys would call me into the kitchen. She would lower herself slowly onto one of the wooden dining chairs, her joints as brittle with arthritis as the creaking, rickety legs of the chair. On the table she would have assembled all the objects of a ritual that has been passed on from black women to black girl children across the generations, across centuries, across the weeping Atlantic. A black wide-toothed comb, a jar of lanolin, some elastic bands in different colors would all be spread out on a white paper napkin. I would sit cross-legged between Aunt Gladys's parted legs, her flowered housecoat hiked up a little so I could see where her stockings had been rolled up just beneath her knees, and see the weave of knotted blue veins under her skin. The air in the kitchen would be saturated with scent: her dry, old-lady skin and the perfumed powder that she wore in her private places, the smoke from her ubiquitous cigarette, the heavy, mineral muskiness of the lanolin, the bittersweet acidity of a pot of greens with onions and vinegar cooking on the stove.

We sit in silence. Aunt Gladys begins to undo my two pigtails, grown fuzzy with sleep and play, and my whole body goes stiff with panic. The combing is next—she takes a section of my loose hair and drags the comb through it, yanking my head back. I howl every time she hits a knot, and there are many, and she has to pull and pull on it with the teeth of the comb until it's gone. *Hush, child,* she hisses, trying to calm me, but my eyes are tearing and my shoulders are cranked up around my ears. I pull my head forward when she begins another section, and she starts to get mad and pulls my head back toward her. This tug-of-war that's so familiar, played out in every kitchen in Harlem, and I'm just another tender-headed child, asserting my will. After the knots are out she parts my hair into four sections, scoops out some lanolin with two fingers and rubs it into my scalp. This, I don't mind. I get quiet again, let my body relax, lean my head back into her lap. After my scalp is greased, she rubs more lanolin into my hair and braids it, using one elastic band at the top of each braid to keep it tight, and another at each end to keep it from unraveling.

Finally Aunt Gladys would let me up and I would bound out of the kitchen and into the bathroom, where I could examine my hair in the mirror. My braids would be smooth and gleaming. The ritual of the hair was both solemn rite and celebration. My hair would be tamed momentarily just as my identity would be fixed, momentarily. In that mirror I would be a six-year-old black girl-child who lived in Harlem. It would be enough, for a time, to hold all the contradictions and questions at bay.

MY MEMORIES OF men from that time are less distinct. There were husbands and boyfriends in the other apartments, men who worked during the day, came home to eat and take a nap, and went back out to another job. Janitor, line cook, night watchman. Relatives who came on weekends bearing groceries. An old man with deeply wrinkled hands and milky eyes who sat on a folding chair in the front courtyard, his cane leaning against the wall. Two or three young boys. Miriam's companion, Charles, who lived with us for a while, barely ever emerging from the living room, where he'd watch baseball games on her color television. The smoke from his cigar spilled down the hall, a viscous, herbaceous, nauseating smell that caught in my throat. Other men were absent, leaving their shadows behind and women waiting. Men like my father who appeared erratically to visit their children, or those I heard Miriam and her friends whisper about, catching only the words "prison" or "the street" or "the bottle."

Uncle Sheldon lived a few blocks away and would come on the weekends to do odd jobs around the house. He had come up to New York from Pittsburgh many years before. I can't picture his face anymore, but I remember a suit he used to wear, light blue with bell-bottom pants. There was a heightening of energy whenever he visited, a lot of laughter, joking, gossip. He and Miriam would sit together and drink cold beer in the kitchen for hours. I would wander in and Uncle Sheldon would pull me up onto his lap, pretend to give me a sip of his beer. He would raise the glass to my mouth, and I would feel the tickle of the foam and smell that sour and sharp odor that I associated with all grown-ups. Miriam would yell at him, but I could tell they weren't serious. I desperately wanted to taste the beer, to share in the secret of it. Miriam would tell me to go to my room, and I'd slide sullenly off Uncle Sheldon's lap, stamping out of the kitchen. Their laughter hung in the air behind me.

One evening, Miriam was putting on her coat to go out, as my mother and I stood with her in the foyer. My mother opened the door for her, unlocked the two deadbolts and the flimsy chain lock. The chain made a clacking sound as it bounced against the metal door. I held on to my mother's leg and watched Miriam walk down the hall—these goodbyes stand out clearly in my mind: Miriam holding me up to kiss my mother before she went out for the night with friends, Miriam or one of my aunts leading me by the hand down the hall to take me to school, me turning around to wave at my mother on the other side of the door. This time we watched as Miriam walked to the stairs—the elevator must have been broken again—and then we heard her screaming. *A man's there,* she cried, and ran back toward the apartment. *I think he's dead!* Miriam went to call the police, and my mother crept down the hall, squinting out at the stairs. In the confusion I followed her. I don't remember feeling afraid, only a vague sense of excitement. My mother stood just at the foot of the stairs, saying, *Oh, God.* I peered around my mother's legs and saw a figure slumped against the short landing just below. I couldn't see his face, but I saw the blood that soaked his clothes and dripped thickly down the steps under him. All this must have happened in a matter of seconds. My mother caught me gaping there, pushed me back into the apartment. Miriam stood at the door, waiting for the police to arrive. She was still wearing her coat, and she was shaking. The sight of my grandmother holding her arms tightly against her body, her chest heaving, filled me with a kind of terror. At my age, the dead man was an abstraction. But this was the first time I had a sense of Miriam's vulnerability. I threw up all over the foyer floor, just as the sound of the police radio echoed up the hallway from somewhere downstairs.

Here is where my memory gets tangled. All my life, I thought it was my Uncle Sheldon on the stairs that night. He was killed around the same time, stabbed to death like that other man. I don't remember when or how Miriam told me, and somehow I've collapsed the two events so that they've formed a single narrative in my mind. Only recently my father told me that I had it wrong. Uncle Sheldon had been killed in some woman's apartment farther uptown—it had been a "crime of passion." Uncle Sheldon was a numbers runner; he had been careless with money and with other men's women, had been in trouble many times. My father told me that he had to go down to the city morgue to identify the body, because neither Miriam nor my mother could bear to do it. My father, whose presence was so random in those days, suddenly man of the family. Miriam never spoke of Uncle Sheldon again. I don't remember any funeral for him, don't know if he was buried in New York or back in Pittsburgh, where almost all of Miriam's family was.

My mother won't talk about him, either. *Why do you want to bring up all those negative things?* she asks, as always exasperated by my need to grasp on to our past, to make some sense of it. *I'm not interested in what went on before—it's over.* Memory for her is an irritation, a waste of time. She simply refuses to acknowledge the past, refuses its claims on her. The present is the only thing that matters to my mother, and the future is the only thing worth wondering about. The future is where things can still turn out right. You can't be distracted, or you might miss it when it finally comes. My mother can't imagine why I would want to root into all those murky places in our history. To her, pain is a fixed and finite thing in time, without amplification or repercussions in the present and beyond. Sometimes I wish I could will away the past the way she can, not answer its call. Sometimes my longing for answers feels shameful, a sordid habit. All my questions just lead to more questions. There is no way I'll ever get clean.

ONCE WHEN I was in high school and in the habit of wearing black dresses from thrift stores, Miriam pulled from her closet a garment bag and what seemed like yards of plastic from the dry cleaner's; inside was a dress that had belonged to my great-grandmother Mae in the 1920s. The dress was black silk with jet beads sewn into the bodice; it was musty and had small tears at the neckline. The black had faded so that it took on a dark green tinge, like something pulled from the bottom of the sea. Miriam wrapped it back up quickly—it was far too fragile for me to try on, to pull up over my combat boots as I did with other people's grandmother's clothes from the secondhand shops along Columbus Avenue. Mae had been a flapper, a preposterously glamorous figure in Homewood, the working-class neighborhood in Pittsburgh where her family had lived for generations. She always wore bright red lipstick and had a glass of Rheingold beer in her hand, even when I knew her as an old woman.

Mae had gone up to New York often during the time of the Harlem Renaissance. She went to parties and jazz clubs, and prowled the shops along 125th Street. She would be gone for months at a time, leaving with one beau and returning with another, one of whom became Miriam's father. When Mae wasn't traveling she lived with her parents, Momma and Poppa, and her four sisters in Homewood. As a girl, Miriam stayed with the extended family and imagined her mother dressed in fine clothes, dancing the Charleston in Harlem with Langston Hughes. When Miriam was in elementary school she copied Hughes's poem "The Negro Dreams of Rivers" and kept it with her, pasted into her diary, wherever she went. She told me later that she knew even then that she wanted to be a writer, and that she wanted to live in Harlem, where everything was happening. By the time she was old enough to imagine this kind of future for herself, though, Harlem was beginning its long decline. After the stock market crash of 1929 the champagne didn't flow so freely in its nightclubs anymore, and many of its writers had moved on to other places. During the Depression the factories, shops, and restaurants that had employed so many people in the neighborhood began to close. In the following decades white landlords began to abandon their buildings or set them on fire to escape their obligations to their tenants and to the IRS, and middle-class black people moved to other parts of the city, taking their businesses with them.

Mae's stories never mentioned the painful realities that had overtaken Harlem; instead it existed for her, and for her impressionable daughter, in an eternal present of tuxedo-clad trumpet players and pale yellow chorus girls, literary salons in grand apartments, women in furs strolling down Lenox Avenue. Mae had always followed the good times, from Harlem to St. Louis, Washington, D.C., to Chicago. Along the way, she had found, and then unburdened herself of, five husbands. She and Miriam's father had split up—it's not clear if they had ever been officially married—after a couple of years. All I know about him is that his mother was African American and Native American from the Powhatan nation in Virginia—Miriam would always boast that we were related through her to both Wayne Newton and Pocahontas. *One day I'm going to Vegas so I can tell Wayne Newton we're cousins,* she would threaten at least once each year.

I also know that Miriam's father's father was Chinese, but I haven't been able to find any record of this man, no name, no photograph. The only information I have about him comes from Miriam and my mother's competing stories: Miriam said that he came from China and had a laundry in Washington, D.C., which she had once visited; my mother insists that he had been a "coolie" in Jamaica and had later laid railroad tracks somewhere in the South. He exists as a fantasy now, the only trace of his presence in the dark, upturned eyes he passed on to Miriam, my mother, and me.

Miriam had seen her own father sporadically throughout her childhood. She always called him by his full name, Benny Holmes. *Benny Holmes called today and asked about you,* she'd say to my indifferent mother, or the one time I met him, *We're going to Washington to visit Benny Holmes.* Miriam called her mother by her first name, and it always seemed to me that Mae was more like a big sister to her. This relationship has repeated itself down through the generations from Mae to Miriam, Miriam to my mother, my mother to me: each had a daughter very young, each struggled to find some independent life for herself outside of motherhood as her daughter looked on from a distance. A dowry of beauty and envy, wild desire and crushed expectations, passed on from one to the other.

EVERY SUMMER, Miriam would take me to visit Mae and the rest of the family in Pittsburgh. Mae had come back to Homewood from her travels and was living in a home for the elderly—a highrise on the corner of an intersection, with an overgrown lot across the street. I'll never forget the address: 7030 Kelly Street. Miriam and I would emerge from the Greyhound station in the early morning, irritable and slightly ill after the long trip from New York and the stale, smoky air inside the bus. *7030 Kelly Street,* Miriam would say sleepily to the jitney cabdriver. I dreaded the arrival at Mae's building, the desolation around it—not a park or a playground in sight—the bleak, empty terraces and the cinderblock walls. There always seemed to be someone being brought out to an ambulance just as we got there, sometimes in a wheelchair, sometimes on a stretcher covered with a white sheet.

Mae had made the apartment as colorful as she could, with a bright red mohair couch and a white wicker chair, each loaded with faded silk pillows with maps of states or islands and embroidered messages like *Wish You Were Here.* The concrete floors were covered with rugs woven from scraps of colored cloth—they were darkened with a year's worth of grime and dust, and Miriam would take them up and wash them by hand within the first day or two of our visit. Miriam spent much of our time there cleaning, washing clothes, filling the refrigerator with food, cooking meals. Mae would sit at her small round dining table and watch, beer in hand, telling Miriam the latest gossip from the building: who died, who remarried at eighty, which apartment was free—maybe there would be a way for Miriam to move in. *Oh, really?* Miriam would call from the kitchen. *How about that.*

I would sit at the table as well, wanting to be close to Miriam, bored already after a couple of days. Mae would ask me about school as I read and reread the comics in the newspaper. *You're such a pretty little girl,* she'd say to me, *just like your mother.* Displayed on the coffee table was a framed picture of my mother in a thick poncho and a straight wig with bangs that partially covered her eyes, cut out of a spread on last year's winter fashions from a New York paper that Miriam had sent her. On the wall beside her bed, Mae had hung a picture of Miriam as a young woman, laughing, her head thrown back into the sunlight.

Beauty seemed to be the topic that each conversation between Mae and Miriam circled back toward, no matter what they were originally talking about. *Didn't Miriam look just like a movie star?* Mae would ask me, gesturing to another picture of Miriam as a high school student in the 1940s, wearing a demure dress that grazed just above her knees, her hair blazing red even in the black and white of the image. *Your great-grandma Mae was some looker when she was young, she drove all the men crazy,* Miriam would echo. *That Alana does have a pretty face,* Mae would say of one of her nieces, *even though she got her father's dark skin.* The stigma of skin of color. The thing that hung in the undercurrent of those conversations in Mae's apartment, though it always found a way to bubble up to the surface.

Mae was the second eldest of five sisters. Their parents were both descended from Homewood's mixed community of free African Americans and early German immigrants, the two groups having lived side by side for generations. By the time I had begun visiting my relatives in Homewood, the neighborhood had grown into a solidly black community. But the corporeal traces of earlier integration and miscsegenation would remain. One of the few official documents I've uncovered is a 1930 census record that describes the household both Mae and Miriam grew up in. Mae's parents, Momma and Poppa, are listed as "homemaker" and "laborer," respectively. In the box marked for race there had been a "W" (white)—the "W" was crossed out at some point and "Neg" (Negro), was scrawled into the remaining space. Miriam had the only existing photograph of Momma, which she kept on top of the dresser in her bedroom. It was color-tinted in a heavy silver frame. Momma looks like a white woman, with shiny blond hair and crinkling blue eyes. She has a broad, plain face and a closed-mouthed smile that tilts slightly to one side, a humble, honest face. The census-taker must have assumed when Momma opened the door that she was indeed white, until she invariably corrected him. He would have then counted Momma's five daughters: Ada—pale-skinned with straight brown hair—the eldest, who would soon marry and move to a house a few blocks away; Virginia, Gladys, and Hazel, like their mother, each blond with blue or green eyes; and Mae, the darkest, with tan skin and black hair. "Neg" is marked in the race box for all of them. Miriam kept a picture of Mae next to the one of Momma on her bedroom dresser; it was a smaller photograph in a cherrywood frame, showing Mae in a party dress and a lavishly tilted wide-brimmed hat. Her dark eyes and spit-curled hair gleam, her lips are painted and parted in an ironic smile. The photograph had been torn across the middle and then pasted back together. I never knew who it was that ripped it or who salvaged it. At the bottom of the picture Mae had written, *lovengly yours, Mae.* I used to spend hours staring at those two photographs, dreaming up lives for each woman, mother and daughter, so different from each other. I think about the pictures now, lost after Miriam's death. With their light skin and straight hair and Mae's crooked spelling, these women were the embodiment of the margins, of the in-between space that I, too, would inhabit.

Mae was a marked woman. Marked by the pigment in her skin, which set her apart, especially from her blond mother and sisters and ultimately from her own light-skinned, red-haired daughter. Mae's difference—her blackness—was relative, of course. She would never know the hardships that her dark-skinned neighbors faced every day. *People mistook her for Spanish or Italian,* Aunt Gladys would tell me proudly. That double-edged pride that I could never understand. Their African heritage was both emblem of honor and source of deep shame. White people—Mae always called them "crackers"—were both feared and ridiculed. Yet to look like them was a great and lucky thing. The family belonged to a caste whose borders were policed shamefully, brutally. One day, I must have been about thirteen, Miriam and I were in the kitchen unloading groceries from a couple of paper shopping bags. She held up one of the bags against her face. *In Pittsburgh there were parties where you couldn't get in if your skin was darker than this bag.* Other times there would be a fine-toothed comb hanging above the door. You weren't allowed in if the comb couldn't be run through your hair.

Yet Miriam was emphatic about her family's refusal to pass for white. Passing was both unimaginable exile and deeply shameful. *We pitied the ones who left,* she told me. I could never tell if she felt—as many African Americans do—that people who passed betrayed the black community, or if she was simply baffled that anyone would choose to live in the bland world of white people.

Yet Miriam also spoke of passing as a temporary economic strategy—in cases of necessity it was understood and tolerated by the community. She remembered a woman who lived down the block in Homewood, whose husband had died years before, who would go to work each morning at a department store across town that only hired white people. In the evenings she'd return to her black neighborhood and cook dinner for her five children. This woman worked in the store's basement, in the bargain shoe department— none of her coworkers suspected she was black. Miriam would shop there sometimes, looking for cheap party shoes. She was always careful not to acknowledge her neighbor in any way, so as not to blow her cover—she'd go to another saleswoman instead. Everyone in the neighborhood knew the woman's secret and kept it safe, because she always came back home.

Mae would have just made it into those paper-bag parties, but once inside she would have felt men's eyes passing quickly from her to her golden sisters. Not only was she the dark one in this setting, but she was fast and reckless, too. She danced and drank and swore like a sailor, and had more lovers than anyone could count. In her pale, hardworking, churchgoing family, this wildness must have been associated with her darkness, as if her visible African blood were an announcement, and indeed the cause, of her moral lapses. I think my great-grandmother Mae's rebellion grew out of this emotional exile—in rebelling, she became the very thing that her skin was supposed to determine.

As a girl, I saw little sign of Mae's early glamour. With age she had grown heavy, waddled from side to side as she made her way around the Kelly Street apartment. Her steel-gray hair hung in two thin braids, and she wore an old, frayed housecoat. Many years before, she had been in a fight with her last husband. He had punched her in the nose, and she had smashed a chair over his head. Mae's broken nose had never properly set, but had healed as a fleshy, bulbous mound—I used to call her Bozo under my breath when I was angry with her. This image of her as a hellcat, a brawler, was something I took for granted, passed on to me by the Pittsburgh aunts and by Miriam. It seemed a joke—oh, your Great-Grandma Mae's so tough, she can take anything. No one ever called her fights with the men in her life abuse.

As an old woman, Mae spent her weekdays drinking, first in the beer garden down the street, and later, when it became more difficult for her to move around, alone at home. Sundays she would put on her best suit and go to church. There would invariably come a point during those summer visits when she and Miriam would get into arguments, shouting at each other from opposite ends of the small apartment. I never understood what they were fighting about. Sometimes we would have to leave early, Miriam packing my little suitcase in the middle of the night and calling a cab to take us back to the bus station. Mae would sit on her wicker chair, arms crossed tightly at her chest, her back turned to us as we walked out the door.

I could never connect the old lady I visited so unwillingly, in her apartment that smelled of death, with the gorgeous, defiant woman in the photograph on Miriam's dresser. I wonder now if Mae's ferocity, the hungry way she tore at life, her rages as an old woman, were like a second skin, a kind of protection against the judgment she might have seen in the eyes of the people closest to her. Against the fear that her daughter's light skin would take her away, into a world of acceptance and belonging that had always eluded her. Mae died when I was in high school. I had long stopped going to Pittsburgh to visit her, though Miriam still went for a few weeks each year. I remember Miriam on the telephone at home in New York, making the funeral arrangements, calling the few remaining relatives to organize a reception. I don't know why I didn't go with her to Pittsburgh. Maybe the funeral was in the middle of a school week, maybe I had exams. The day she left I watched Miriam put on a black dress—I had never seen her in black before. She bustled around the house, making sure there was enough food in the refrigerator, sweeping the floors, writing out checks for the bills. I hadn't seen her cry once since we got the news about Mae's death. I thought of Miriam alone on the bus that night, her coat on top of her to keep away the chill of the air-conditioning, staring out the window at the cars speeding down the highway.

I don't remember the first time Miriam told me about Sybela Owens, our first known ancestor. My knowledge of her seems to have been with me always, passed down from the fragments that Miriam learned as a child and later embellished for me, each generation passing the story down as if through the blood. Sybela Owens—a black woman enslaved on a plantation in Maryland in the mid-1800s—was the grandmother of Miriam's grandmother, Momma. Miriam described her as very young and mulatta—the man who originally owned her was probably her father. As a young girl, she had been sold to another plantation—soon after, the new plantation master's son began coming to her cabin at night. She gave birth to two pale children. The master's son grew attached to the little family, to the child mother and the babies he forced from her body. His father worried over the time he was spending with Sybela—he had not found a wife of his own, and seemed to have no intention of looking. Finally, the father arranged to have Sybela and the children sold off, each to a different plantation. Here Miriam would always lower her voice and give a kind of conspiratorial, sideways look, as if to make sure no one would hear what happened next.

Late one night, the plantation owner's son came into the cabin, told Sybela to pack up her few belongings. They each picked up a child, and they ran. A great forest once covered the hills between Maryland and Pennsylvania—the four of them spent days running through it, hiding at night among the trees, gathering food wherever they found it. They ended up in the industrial city of Pittsburgh, and were among the first settlers in Homewood, the neighborhood where Miriam grew up. There are no surviving photographs of Sybela Owens—perhaps none were ever taken—but Miriam had an image of her based on her mother's memory of seeing her as a child: a silent old woman in a long dress, sitting in a rocking chair, alone on the porch of a house in Homewood. This image has floated down over the years like a dream, passed on from one woman to another, a dream of our birth and our survival.

Yet even as Sybela is the axis on which the whole of our family history turns, I could never find *her* in the story. Over the years I would ask Miriam to tell me again about Sybela—I wanted to know who she was. Miriam spoke of the flight through the forest not as escape, but as theft—*the plantation owner's son kidnapped Sybela,* she would tell me each time. As if Sybela didn't want to leave the plantation, had never dreamed of running away herself. In the story, at least the way I grew up hearing it, the white man sets everything in motion by taking her. His actions are clear and even his emotions are implied—fear, lust, some kind of love. But what about Sybela? What did she feel? What did she want? And why have we displaced her over the generations, reduced her to the passivity of a stolen article of property?

So I imagine. Imagine her flight. When the white man opens the cabin door, Sybela has already gathered up a few essentials, pulled the children from their sleep. They have been planning this moment for months, ever since he told her the news that his father was going to sell her and the children. She has endured many things in her brief life: untold hours laboring for white people in their white mansions, scrubbing their dirty clothes, serving their endless courses of food, cleaning their chamber pots. She has been cursed by plantation mistresses enraged by the similarity of her skin to their own, helpless at the sight of so many nearly white children in the fields, the scullery, and the slave quarters who look just like their husbands. She has been raped by one white man who tells her that he loves her as he pushes his way into her night after night—most likely others have tried the same thing, perhaps her own father among them. All this she has survived, but she will not tolerate being torn away from her children.

Sybela looks around the cabin one more time, the only home she's known all her adult life, the only space of relative safety she could provide for her children. A low wooden shack, a couple of straw mattresses on the floor covered with quilts that she made from old work clothes and bits of fancy fabric the children's father brought her from town. This is where she closed her eyes and relinquished her body to yet another form of labor demanded of her. This is where her two yellow children were born, a boy and a girl.

Sybela and the white man would have each carried a child, and small bundles with the few provisions he would have stolen from his father's house—a loaf of bread, some cheese, a little dried meat. They crossed out of the plantation in silence, hushing the sleepy children when they grumbled for their beds. Sybela and the white man ran through the night, feeling their way through the tangle of leaves and branches, brambles and streams that surrounded them, wondering how close behind the master's men and their hounds would be, wondering if they would really make it to the other side.

Shards of story, a gathering of bits of memory and conversation cobbled into the narrative of Sybela's flight to freedom, and of the birth of my family. The details that Miriam remembered from her own childhood speak of the intricate crossings of blood, class, and culture that made us what we are: hybrids, shapeshifters, tresspassers. Sybela's original owner's name had been Auen, they were Germans who had changed their name to Owen to fit in among their Yankee neighbors. Her children's father's family had come from Ireland two generations before, seeking their fortune in the American South. Her children were born with blue eyes. And what of Sybela's own mother? She remains unnamed, invisible. Where along the way in the transmission of the story did she drop out?

CHAPTER FOUR

Miriam moved from Pittsburgh to Los Angeles as a young bride in the late 1940s, following her actor husband's dreams of Hollywood. There she would pursue her own dream as well: to become a writer. A couple of years after they arrived, she began writing for the society page of one of the city's African American newspapers, the *Los Angeles Eagle*. She covered all the social events of the black upper and middle classes, the actors and singers, the doctors and businessmen, their weddings, debutante parties, charity balls. She wrote about each of these social performances, reflecting and amplifying, as if to prove to this small group that they really existed, that this life was really possible. She kept a few press photographs from that time, glossy black and white headshots and group portraits, in each of them Miriam looking like she had been born to that life. Voluptuous in pale strapless dresses and a wide, ruby-lipped smile, she was dazzling. The other people in the pictures, men with white formal jackets, elegant women holding up wine glasses to toast the camera, were, like Miriam, all light-skinned. Miriam would tell me stories about how her actor friends would get bit parts in Hollywood movies playing exotic background characters; the vagueness of their skin color meant that they were cast as Arab sheikhs, Spanish dancers, Indian squaws.

Miriam's dark-skinned husband, whose own career had never taken off, didn't appear in these pictures. I would be a young woman before she would speak of him to me, before I would ever even see a photograph of this man, my grandfather.

ANOTHER TREASURE from Miriam's closet, that she had brought with her from California to Harlem and finally to the apartment in midtown where she lived at the end of her life: a brown knit poncho and matching skirt that belonged to Marilyn Monroe. Marilyn had been an acquaintance, a friend of a friend Miriam never named. It was the early 1950s, both women were at the beginning of their careers, and the future must have seemed to them a bright field of hope and possibility. Miriam would make pots of chili for Marilyn when they were both broke and hungry. They were the same size, and once they had traded clothes, Miriam ending up with the knit outfit. Of course, she never wore it, but kept it wrapped up along with Mae's flapper dress, artifacts of femininity from other ages, which would later seem to me like objects pulled from different layers of an archaeological excavation. I was struck by how small Marilyn Monroe's clothes were, as though they had belonged to a doll.

Marilyn and Miriam, Miriam and Marilyn, together in some small Southern California bungalow, sitting at a kitchen table with the big pot of chili between them, ravenous. Outside the reach of those other, constant hungers, men's desire and the gaze of the camera. What refuge did they find in each other? I wonder. Marilyn, the world's ideal of female beauty, the blond goddess incarnate. Miriam, almost as light, a fantasy of a certain kind of black womanhood, its value judged by how near it could come to whiteness. I think of them with their hair in curlers, their faces slathered with Pond's cold cream. Their eyes laughing out at each other— one set brown, one set blue—from behind those frothy snow-white masks.

It is 1970. My mother is in her early twenties. Her body is pure voluptuousness and abundance. *Jiggle it over here, baby,* the men yell. One of the iconic, contested images of this period is of women burning their bras in bonfires on the street, going to war to liberate their flesh. However it happens, many women do begin to go out braless, allowing their bodies to breathe, to take their true form in public. Miriam still wears her full-length bras and girdles, the ones that mold her breasts into 1950s torpedoes and pull her hips and belly into a single, manageable mass. My mother has never burned her bras. She's stopped wearing them for more aesthetic reasons, to feel the sensation of her body open to its own movement, for the way she looks when she moves, like a river flowing. Without a bra she's removed yet another layer of mediation that separates her body from itself, the city, the street. Sometimes men try to grab her body, and women shake their heads in disgust at her. But when I look up at her and she smiles at me, squeezes my hand almost imperceptibly, I feel safe, like she has everything under control. I feel a gushing pride that this incandescent being is my mother. And in my own childish way, I want to posess her, as the men want to possess her in theirs. I want to call out to all of them, *She's mine, she belongs to me!*

What is it like to be the daughter of a beautiful woman? Whenever my mother picked me up from school or took me shopping with her, I saw that everyone watched her. Car horns honked at her, men stopped on the street and followed her, women examined her clothes and hair through narrowed eyes. My mother: skin like honey, dark almond eyes, a mouth shaped like a heart, brown hair in a thousand tiny braids that shifted and rustled when she moved, wild forest sounds. When we walked together, I experienced my mother as phenomenon, as movement, shape, color. I was witness to what her body set in motion. I would stumble along, holding her hand, trying to keep up with her long-legged stride. We would be surrounded by the sensations of the city, stoplights changing from green to red, buses heaving their way up and down 125th Street, steam like hot hangover breath hissing from manhole covers. Albert Ayler's saxophone floating out of an open apartment window, the voice of Celia Cruz flashing like fire from a passing car.

When my mother walked down the street swinging her hips and smiling her smile that was both seduction and beatitude, men would call out to her: *Hey, Cleopatra! How are you today, my fine black sister?* She smiled back at them, breathed in their words, their sighs, their longing. *Sister, girlfriend, mama,* they called, familiar words, a common language of relationship, of desire.

For a moment—a slow-motion moment stretched the length of a city block—I see the power of beauty. The power of my mother's eyes and lips and body, and the sunlight and the beating heart of the city and the men's blood boiling. At this moment anything is possible. She is a poem made of skin. At this moment she loves herself and I love her for letting me walk with her. This is the mystery that Miriam and Mae spoke of, pointing to the photographs of their own youth. Beauty was a means of transcending mere survival, it was what the women in my family used to seek

out their own dreams, to live those dreams, however partially and temporarily. As I child I felt certain that I would not grow into beauty, that I would never be able to harness its power for myself. I couldn't believe that I came from my mother's body, which had long ago relinquished its maternal function and was now made solely for desire. Next to her I didn't feel like a comparable miracle, fruit of her womb. I wasn't enough like her—I couldn't possibly belong to her, skinny and yellow as I was, with short, fuzzy pigtails and missing my two front baby teeth. I knew even then that I would have to find another way.

MY MOTHER had a sheepskin coat that she would wear all winter long. I must have been around three or four, but I remember it well. The coat was one of those elaborate, hippie, peasant-chic garments, more costume than utility, that was so popular in the early 1970s. It was a dark lapis blue suede on the outside, covered with flowers embroidered in red and yellow silk. The fleece of the sheep—a yellowish white like old ivory—was on the inside. Its long, curled tendrils smelled of musk, that concentrated, warm presence that I would recognize years later when I walked in the woods for the first time and came upon a spot where a deer had left its scent. In the afternoons, sometimes, my mother would spread the coat out on her bed with the fur on the outside, and let me take a nap on it. I loved the feeling of being snuggled against the fleece, how warm and scratchy it felt against my skin. I would bury my nose deep into all that whiteness, breathe in the sharp animal smell. Somehow I'd imagine myself connected to the life of the sheep this coat once was, feel its spirit watching over me, like an angel.

.   .   .

SOMETIMES MY mother would sit with me and sing to me as I fell asleep. She knew one lullaby, the one Miriam used to sing to her when she was a small child:

> *you are my sunshine*
> *my only sunshine*
> *you make me happy*
> *when skies are gray*

My mother's voice was high and breathy, like a girl's. She sang off-key. But that didn't matter—she was there with me, singing only to me. As my eyes closed I'd feel myself descending, deeper into the white fur, deeper into the sound of her voice and the words she sang. Soon the words grew distant and abstract as falling stars, and I would feel perfectly safe. It's the only time in my life that I would ever feel this way.

THE MOST dangerous place in our building, besides the dark basement where no one ever went, was the elevator. When it wasn't broken it would heave and lurch from floor to floor, its clattering doors never shutting properly. People would get stuck in there for hours; they'd have to bang on the doors and yell until a neighbor would hear them and call the fire department. My mother has told me how much she hated getting into that elevator alone, how usually she avoided it altogether and climbed the five flights of stairs instead. One day she had been too tired to walk. She had just come back from grocery shopping, carrying me in her arms and struggling with bags of food. She remembers that I had just turned a year old. She waited for the elevator, holding me against her hip, the bags resting on the floor. She heard a car horn honking outside, a radio playing somewhere on the second floor. The elevator wouldn't come; she pressed the button again and again, but it seemed stuck on one of the other floors.

A young man came into the building. The lock on the front door was always broken, anyone could come in at any time. My mother says that she wasn't afraid of him at first. They were probably around the same age; he could have been the cousin or boyfriend of one of the neighbors. My mother kept pressing the elevator button; finally it began making its way down to the lobby. The young man smiled at her and she smiled back. He offered to carry her bags into the elevator, and she let him. Men wanted to help her all the time, she had come to expect it by now. In the elevator he made a joke about the smell of piss that hung in the air, the stickiness of the floor. Laughing, at ease, my mother went to press the button for the fifth floor, when suddenly the man turned to her and grabbed me out of her arms. He lifted up his shirt and pulled out a hunting knife that he had stuffed behind his belt, and put the knife to my throat. Only then did my mother notice that his face was covered with sweat, junkie sweat. His eyes were like ice. She didn't know what to do. She remembers how I screamed and reached for her. The elevator began to rise. My mother prayed for someone to get on at another floor, but no one did.

My mother says that she tried to be calm, to talk to him. He told her to give him all her money, but she didn't have any, she had spent it all on food. She went through her purse, her pockets, showed him that she had nothing to give him, pleading with him to give me back to her. On the fifth floor, the elevator doors opened. An old woman who lived down the hall was waiting on the landing. *She must have scared him,* my mother laughs, *because as soon as he saw her, the man shoved you back at me and ran away.* My mother talks about it now in a detached way, like it's a story she's read in a newspaper, just another mugging in Harlem. It's been a long time since she's shown fear, shown any vulnerability at all. But I can imagine her terror at nineteen or twenty, her helplessness in that moment. Her voice disappearing into her throat as she struggled to stay calm, her inability to protect me or herself. And where is this memory stored in me? In what hidden-away space in my mind or my body, what primal baby place? The cold metal on my neck, the adrenaline, the incomprehension.

MY MOTHER has many secrets. I don't know quite how old she is. She tells everyone something different, and even Miriam questioned herself about the exact year she gave birth, such is the power of my mother's talent for evasion. *A woman's age is her own business,* my mother says. This mystery only adds to her glamour, another piece of her that no one will ever own, not even me. She has always looked impossibly young; even now that I am an adult in my thirties, she looks the same to me as when I was a teenager and she was in her thirties. Her skin never seems to wrinkle, and she always colors her hair—sometimes brown, sometimes auburn, most often a lioness blond. I have never seen any sign of gray on her head, never a single coiling defiant strand, like the ones I find now when I look into the mirror. When she does begin to age it happens from the inside out: muscles pulled in her back, bones grown fragile so she fractures her hand after a slip on the ice one winter, painful stones in her gallbladder that have to be removed in an emergency surgery early one summer morning. But on the surface of her, there's never a ripple. And for as long as I can remember I have this feeling of guilt and panic each year around my birthday. If I get older, that means she has to get older, too. At the same time, I look forward to every one of my birthdays, imagine perhaps naively that each year might bring some kind of wisdom, but my mother will have none of it. I imagine that each birthday to her feels like an oncoming Mack truck; it's best to just duck and get out the way. As I get older I feel that truck bearing down on her, closer and closer.

Yet she has always gone out of her way to make my own birthdays a real celebration. There were a few years in elementary school when she arranged huge parties for me at a western-themed restaurant downtown. All my classmates would be invited; after our meal of hamburgers and birthday cake we would be taken for rides around the block in a replica of a stagecoach. I felt like the most special, most loved child in the world. Later she would take me to grown-up dinners at fancy restaurants, or give me a good watch or money toward a vacation. I know now that much of the time she could hardly afford these extravagances. Yet she rarely accepts my adult efforts to celebrate her birthday, to bring it out into the light. *I don't even want to think about it,* she'll say, half jokingly.

There's something else that no one knows about her. My mother has a genius-level IQ. Miriam had kept the score of the IQ test my mother took as a child in a manila envelope, along with a pile of certificates of merit and her high school diploma. At two and a half my mother was already beginning to read. She could count much earlier than other children as well, reciting numbers to herself in her room, additions and subtractions instead of nursery rhymes. Once they got to Harlem, Miriam put my mother into private school; she didn't trust the public schools in New York, not with the great potential of her daughter's mind. Much of her income would go toward paying whatever my mother's many scholarships couldn't cover, as my mother's money would later be poured into my own private school education.

When I asked her, my mother didn't remember anything about

the test itself, where it happened, if it was difficult, how she felt when it was over. I see her sitting at a desk in her blue school uniform, with her knee socks and her patent-leather shoes that she kept perfectly shined. Her perfectly sharpened pencil, and the paper in front of her. The other children taking the test that day, all white. The large institutional clock on the wall at the front of the room staring down at her blankly. She twists one of her stiff, beribboned pigtails around her finger and gets to work. I can envision the scene, but can't get hold of what she might have been feeling. My mother's emotions, even at six or seven, are a locked door. She simply did what she was told. She took the test and received a number: 160. The same as Einstein.

My mother went to an Episcopalian high school in the Bronx. She took the subway by herself, there and back each day. She doesn't remember the name of the school, or where it was exactly. I wonder if it was anywhere near the neighborhood my father lived in, if they had ever passed each other on the train. Would my father at fifteen or sixteen already have been looking beyond the confines of his neighborhood for another kind of life, another way to love? Would his head have been turned even then by a beautiful black girl in a prim school uniform? My mother does remember that the students were mostly of German descent; she was one of the only black students. I ask her if she ever felt racism from the other students toward her. Had she been threatened, ostracized? I picture her with her books held tightly against her chest, sitting quietly in the back of the room, trying not to call attention to herself. But it's me I'm seeing in that classroom forty years ago, not her. *Not at all,* my mother says brightly. *I was homecoming queen.* She even had a white boyfriend, an actual German with ice-blond hair and glittering blue eyes. He was an exchange student, she's long forgotten his name. They went to the prom together, and then he had to go back to Germany. My mother in a ball gown, a crown sparkling atop her head, dancing in the center of the gymnasium floor with her Teutonic date. This image says everything about her: a baffling combination of defiance and conformity, vulnerability and pure will.

Along the way, she had skipped two grades, and graduated from high school just before her seventeenth birthday. After the IQ test, Miriam had begun to dream great things for my mother, imagining her going to Harvard, becoming a scientist, a doctor, or a lawyer. She must have believed that my mother's intelligence would transcend her beauty and her race. *Your mother could have done anything she wanted with her life,* Miriam would say to me through the years, an idea she had believed in fiercely. But the *anything she wanted* part was always qualified; it meant getting a degree and living what Miriam saw as a respectable life for a black woman of their caste. My mother was already making her own way, though, improvising a life for herself that was unrecognizable to Miriam.

After high school my mother got a job as a secretary. There were vague plans for her to work for a year and decide where she'd like to go to college. Miriam told me that my mother had even visited a few campuses, though she couldn't remember which ones. Soon my mother met my father, and a short time later, Miriam's worst nightmare came true. My mother says that there was simply no time to go back to school. I had been born; soon she was working two jobs to support us. But I think she never seriously considered going to college. She always hated confinement of any kind; she says that even as a dutiful schoolgirl, she couldn't wait for the last bell to ring. The rigid structure of academic life, having to sit in the same room at the same time each day, had been a struggle from the beginning. She loved learning and information, but wanted to consume and interpret it in her own way, on her own time.

Indeed, my mother has always read hungrily, promiscuously, everything from Hermann Hesse to Jacqueline Susann. It was a habit that began in elementary school; whenever she would do well on a test or a paper, Miriam would buy her a book. Miriam, too, had taken shelter in books all her life. She had one huge bookcase that leaned and groaned with its load of novels and histories in a corner of the living room in Harlem. Her favorites—the collected plays of Shakespeare, the poems of her beloved Langston Hughes, Edith Hamilton's *Mythology*—were always proudly displayed on the middle shelf, just at eye level if you were seated on the couch next to the bookcase. Later, when Miriam began taking evening classes at New York University, she would add to that group of favorites Plato's *Republic* and Laurence Sterne's *Tristram Shandy*.

Whenever my mother had a day off, she would go alone to the public library. She'd take out a pile of books and read them all within the week; this remains one of the constants in her life. In the mornings before work, or in the evenings when she didn't have a date, she would be stretched out on the couch, a book in her hands, her black, cat's-eye reading glasses perched on the tip of her nose. This is the image I love best of my mother, that rare moment of stillness and almost devout concentration she has when she's lost in a book. I've always thought that these are the times when she is truly at peace, when she is out of reach of the grasping fingers of the outside world. I wonder now if the love Miriam and my mother had for books, the solace they both found in them, was something they could share. Did they talk to each other about what they read, my mother's delight in the intricacies of plot, Miriam's fascination with the power and beauty of language itself?

Or was it simply something Miriam passed on to her daughter, a basic fact, like family resemblance, that each carried in her own separate way? The two of them sharing an apartment, each inhabiting the book she was reading, alone, keeping her pleasure and her insight to herself?

MIRIAM HAD HER own secrets. If my mother carries her secrets deep within her body, Miriam kept hers hidden, literally, in her closet. I was thirty years old when she showed me a photograph of my grandfather for the first time. It was a Sunday morning in August, at her apartment on 58th Street. I remember that her telephone wasn't working. The night before there had been a violent storm, the kind of storm that is specific to New York in August, sudden and vengeful. In the morning the sky was a placid blue, contrite like a child after a temper tantrum. I had come over early, bringing bagels and the Sunday paper, our weekly ritual.

I open all the windows in the house, let in the fresh, cool air. Miriam and I are always arguing about fresh air; she wants the windows closed tight. The sweetness of the new air mingles with the heavy scent of coffee Miriam is brewing in the tiny kitchen. *What was my mother's father like?* I call out to her as I begin to set the table. This is a question I've never asked before, and I don't know what makes me ask it now, on this clear morning. My mother's father—Miriam never referred to him as her ex-husband—was a taboo subject. All I ever heard about him—and this just once—was his name, Samuel Stevens. It was almost as if he had never existed. I grew up never giving him any thought; it was the women's stories that endlessly fascinated me, and in the women's stories men seemed to have little besides walk-on parts.

There is no response from the kitchen. *Did you hear me? What was he like?* And she doesn't answer. I go into the kitchen—she's not there. I can hear rustling sounds coming from her bedroom. I follow them and find her going through the bags in her closet. *It's here somewhere,* she says quietly without turning around. Finally she pulls out a torn manila envelope and sits on her bed. The closet door is open and all the bags, there must be twenty of them piled up on top of each other, are in complete disarray. I sit down next to her as she pulls two photographs from the envelope. The first is a large sepia portrait. The paper it's printed on is porous and cracked with age. Miriam is on the left, her hair pulled back in a low chignon, its shine exaggerated by the way the light is falling. She's wearing a dark dress with a lace collar and jeweled clip-on earrings. Next to her is my mother as a toddler. She looks about one year old, her eyes are wide and glistening, and she's looking into the camera as if she's responding to something that's happening outside the frame. I imagine that the photographer is holding up a puppet or making a funny face, something to capture her attention, to occupy her mind that is already flashing and crackling, long before the IQ test and the expectations for her future.

To the right of my mother is a man. The first thing I notice about him is his incredibly sweet face. He has a smile like a boy's, almost shy. There is a look of pride in his eyes. He has dark skin and close-cropped hair, and he's wearing a suit and tie. So this is my grandfather. I look again from his face to Miriam's and then back to my mother, trying to map the resemblance. She has Miriam's full lips, and her skin is somewhere in between Miriam's and her father's. I try to imagine them as a family, to read happiness in the composition of the image, the chemistry of the print. Miriam is not smiling. Her face is like a white mask. She looks as though she were at a funeral instead of sitting for a family portrait. Maybe the photographer tried to get her to smile, winked a little at her while he distracted her little daughter. But there is no trace of feeling or recognition in her eyes. Miriam hands me the photograph, traces her finger from her own image to my grandfather's in a smooth line. *He raped me,* she says plainly.

Miriam at sixteen. Honor student, pride of the family, beauty of the neighborhood. She is a serious and obedient girl, spends most of her time studying. Wherever she goes she carries with her a notebook, the fountain pen Poppa gave her for her birthday last year, a ruler for keeping her handwriting straight, and a book from one of her classes at the local high school. Practicing her trigonometry on the bus home after school, catching up before church services, a copy of Thomas Hobbes's *Leviathan* hidden in an open Bible. It's springtime. The trees of Homewood are in bloom, fresh pink and white buds having forced their way through tough winter bark. The air smells of warm soil and clean laundry hanging in backyards; she feels its warmth on her smooth arms now that she doesn't need a jacket.

For the first time, Miriam is in the school play. Momma and Poppa never cared much for theater, and they worried about her being involved in something so frivolous when she should be focusing on her lessons. Besides, it would make her vain, and they wouldn't tolerate vanity in their house. It was a sin, the devil's work. They had prayed for Miriam's own mother, their daughter Mae, when vanity had taken hold of her. But this year the drama club was doing *Romeo and Juliet,* and above all things, Miriam loved Shakespeare. Loved the sound his words made in her mouth. She tried out for the part of Juliet in secret and got it, of course. She was Juliet from the moment she walked into the auditorium, with her pale skin and her long red hair. How many darker-skinned girls longed for the part, imagined themselves as Juliet, alone in their rooms at night? How many darker-skinned girls who knew every breathless, tormented line, who were just as beautiful? At sixteen Miriam didn't think of these things. She worked for this part, and as far as she was concerned, she won it fair and square. For a week she kept the news from Momma and Poppa, and when she told them, they couldn't believe that she had gone against their wishes. Just like Mae, and look where she was now.

Somehow, Miriam convinces them that being in the play will help her be a better student. Something about how Shakespeare was the greatest writer who ever lived, something about extra credit and getting into a good college. Momma and Poppa are practical people. Whatever shred of extra advantage they can scrape from the surface of the white world they offer to Miriam. If she can recite Shakespeare, she can do anything else that white people can do. Then anything will be possible for her, won't it?

Miriam stays up late every night learning her lines. She wakes up in the morning with the memory of Elizabethan English imprinted on her tongue. At breakfast she begins to drink the sweet, strong coffee with chicory that Momma roasts fresh, pushing away her usual glass of milk for caffeine's gradual opening and heightening of the senses. Momma serves her biscuits and gravy in anxious silence, Poppa peers at her from behind his newspaper, as if he could see proof of cultural edification somewhere on her face. Miriam picks at her breakfast while she reviews a chapter in a textbook, and then rushes off to school.

Rehearsals are after class in the auditorium. She loves this time, when the school goes quiet and the only people around are the students in the drama club—the actors and the crew—and the drama teacher, the sweet-faced Mr. Stevens. Miriam had seen him in the hallways at school, mysterious and distinguished in his black corduroy blazer and open-collared shirts. A real artist. Samuel Stevens is in his late twenties. He arrived in Pittsburgh from a mountain town in North Carolina, where the people had been mixed, black and Cherokee, for generations. He came to find work in the steel mills, though he dreamed of being an actor. The mills were hot and loud, every night he came home with the echo of machines pounding inside his head. He had quit inside of a year and began working odd jobs while he studied acting with a white teacher downtown who didn't mind giving lessons to coloreds—all money was green, after all. But there aren't a lot of roles for a black man in the theaters of Pittsburgh, and he can't afford to move to one of the bigger cities like New York or Chicago, not just yet. As a last resort he applies for the job of drama coach at Miriam's high school, and to his surprise he gets it.

Miriam moons over Samuel Stevens silently while she stands on the makeshift balcony, calling down to the boy who plays Romeo—what was his name? Below her the other actors are going over their lines in the wings, and backstage, girls who didn't get a part are sewing costumes of red velvet and lace, Miriam's Juliet gown among them. The air is thick with the set-builders' sawdust and the mildew that clings to the stage curtains. Up on her balcony, Miriam feels movement all around her, feels that she is the center of it all, feels beautiful, a rose by another name. She doesn't see Samuel Stevens watching her, taking her in, her youth, her woman's body, her lips that she tints with rouge in the girls' bathroom before each rehearsal, hoping he'll notice her.

One day he asks Miriam if she can come to an extra rehearsal, on a Saturday afternoon. They'll work at his house, where there will be no distractions—Saturdays the glee club meets in the auditorium. He tells her that she needs some work on her final monologue, and she doesn't know whether to be honored by his offer for extra help or crushed that she hasn't learned the part perfectly by now. Still, she tells Momma and Poppa that she's going to the library, slips out before they see that she's wearing her best Sunday dress. She takes the bus to his apartment on the other side of town, working her monologue under her breath like an incantation the whole way there.

Almost a half a century later, Miriam's memory blurs. She tells me that she can remember arriving at his house, sitting on the couch, drinking lemonade. Then everything is blank. She woke up and it was dark outside. Her dress was pulled up around her waist. There was blood—

She didn't tell anyone what happened. She didn't believe it herself. She had only kissed a couple of boys on her doorstep after the rare date Momma and Poppa would allow, all she knew about sex was what was cryptically alluded to in hygiene class. Samuel Stevens had given her a napkin to clean herself up, and then drove her home in silence. Miriam doesn't remember what she told Momma and Poppa when she came in so late, doesn't remember missing her period the following month, or the next. Only that her belly started to push out against her clothes. She dropped out of *Romeo and Juliet*, fell behind in her schoolwork. Momma and Poppa were unusually calm when she finally told them. It was as if their fears for her had been confirmed the day she tried out for the play. This was simply the denouement of a story that had already been written. Poppa rounded up some of his buddies, big workingmen, and broke down the door of Samuel Stevens's apartment. They brought him back to the house dazed and bloody, forced him onto his knees on the living room floor. Momma brought Miriam downstairs, held her hand while Samuel Stevens begged for her forgiveness and promised to marry her.

After the school term ended, Miriam and Samuel Stevens were joined in lawful union in a civil ceremony. My mother was born a few months later. They stayed in Homewood, in a rented apartment, until Miriam finished high school the following year. Momma watched my mother while Miriam was in class.

This is how I imagine the story. A Pittsburgh tragedy. The truth is, all I have are a handful of facts or half-remembered images: the drama club, Miriam's dress pulled up, the marriage. What memories Miriam did have about her life at that time and about her relationship with Samuel Stevens stayed locked away in her closet, somewhere where I'd never reach them. Was the play *Romeo and Juliet,* or have I heard this story somewhere before, read it in another book, seen it on some made-for-TV movie? A handful of facts like bones found at a hidden burial site, the scene of a crime that happened so long ago they've stopped looking for the body. Yet it's precisely this body that I want to resurrect, Miriam's girlhood body made of dreams and promise and hope. I build a story around what's been forgotten to bring flesh back to the bones. I want to give Miriam her childhood back.

And then there is that other thing: beauty. How with Miriam and my mother, beauty overran them. It was not a special gift, like intelligence. It was something monstrous, a thing that made them lonely, that seemed to predetermine their actions and the actions of others, a thing that set uncontrollable stories in motion, that would both precede them and follow them like a curse. In fact, both sides of my family believed in curses: my Italian relatives called it *il malocchio,* the evil eye. A curse that would be put on you by someone who envied you for what you had, or for what you looked like. Black folks called it bad luck. The worst bad luck came from mirrors, if you dropped one, presumably because you were gazing at yourself too long and got distracted. If the mirror broke, the shards strewn at your feet, reflecting your startled image back at you in pieces, bad luck would follow you for seven years.

Miriam left Samuel Stevens after seven years of marriage, seven years of silence and barely contained rage and her face becoming that white mask. They had moved out to Los Angeles soon after Miriam graduated from high school. She had given up on her plans to go to college—how could she, with a small child to care for, a husband to feed, a house to run? She turned to writing in what spare time she could gather. Within a year she had begun to work freelance for the local black newspaper, and slowly she put aside money, a little each week, until she had enough for a Greyhound bus ticket to New York City. Children rode for free.

That morning after the storm, Miriam told me one more thing about Samuel Stevens. She handed me another photograph, also black and white, small enough to fit in the palm of my hand. It was my mother sitting on a lawn in a cowgirl outfit. *Samuel Stevens tried to be a good husband,* she told me. *He loved your mother like nobody's business, and he tried to love me, too.* He worked as a porter in a hotel during the day, teaching acting in the evenings to other aspiring black actors. Bought Miriam jewelry and flowers, took her out to dinner on Friday nights. They had friends and a house full of activity, rehearsals for new plays, parties, political meetings. But after seven years, he and Miriam were worn out, ground down by his increasingly desperate attempts to win her love and the immovable force of her refusal. When Miriam left him, he stayed in Los Angeles for a few years, holding on to the vague career he believed he was making for himself. Eventually the acting jobs stopped coming, and he moved back to Pittsburgh. I don't know what happened to him there, or whether he's dead or alive.

I am oddly comforted by the idea of him struggling for redemption. It makes him human, this man who was my grandfather. And it helps me to try to write this story without shame. Shame at how light skin and beauty were equated in the lives of the women in my family. How Miriam came to believe that light skin somehow made you not only special but also vulnerable to predation, how she didn't completely admit to the immense privilege that came with it. Shame that the violence and absence of Samuel Stevens coexist with the fact that he had dark skin. How can I write these words and not reinforce the usual stereotypes of dangerous black men and fragile, tragic mulattas? Who might this story hurt? Who might it heal?

And then I look down at the photograph in my palm, the image of my mother sitting on the grass, smiling. She's wearing a miniature ten-gallon hat, tied under her chin with ribbon, and shiny new cowboy boots. I look closer. She's holding a kitten. Miriam tells me that it was my mother's third birthday, taken just before her party, and that what you can't see in the frame is the pony that Samuel Stevens had rented for the afternoon. My beautiful mother is the child of these two people brought together by desire, the innocence and violence of it. A light-skinned woman and a dark-skinned man. And my mother was loved, deeply, by them both. This is the truth.

SOON AFTER she had moved to New York, Miriam had found a job reporting for the *Amsterdam News,* again writing articles on the public lives of socially prominent African Americans. After her death, the editor of that paper wrote her obituary. It describes Miriam's work there, and also the other jobs she had during the decades she lived in Harlem. In the early 1960s, she left her job at the *Amsterdam News* and had become a public relations consultant for local businesses, including a popular nightspot, Wells Famous Restaurant, known for its extravagant dinners of fried chicken and waffles. The obituary says that Miriam became the manager of Wells and transformed a vacant space above the restaurant into a successful jazz club. Yet the published history of the club describes it as a major institution in Harlem since 1938, when Miriam was just a schoolgirl, still dreaming of the day she'd come to live in Harlem. I grew up hearing stories about Wells Famous Restaurant from Miriam; she loved especially to tell me about the night that Sammy Davis, Jr., and Kim Novak, who were lovers at the time, had dinner there with Frank Sinatra. *People would come from all over the world to eat at Wells,* Miriam would tell me, her breath catching a little, the way it always did when she was deep into a story, as if she had to come up for air. *It was the most exciting place to be in those days.* She'd talk about how she used to throw parties there in honor of local celebrities, and organize fundraisers to support black politicians. Yet I haven't come across any other record of her presence there besides the obituary; her name isn't mentioned in any article about Wells and its history that I've been able to find.

This was before I was born, when Miriam was still the glamorous woman of those L.A. photographs, the woman who wore fancy dresses and drank champagne. This was the mother my own mother knew when she was a young girl. She must have watched Miriam get dressed for her evenings out, stood beside her as she put on her lipstick at the small mirror above the sink in the bathroom, worked her sore, black-stockinged feet into a pair of high-heeled shoes. Just as I would watch my own mother, mesmerized, almost two decaes later.

The Miriam I grew up with was different. The obituary features a photograph of her from around 1970; she still has that broad, lipsticked smile, but her hair is cut short; she's wearing a necklace made of chunky wooden beads and a dress with a modest

neckline. At this point, she was working in city politics, campaigning for Democrats in various elections. There was a framed photograph in the apartment in Harlem—I remember it well from that
time, although I don't know what happened to it after we left—of
Miriam sitting on our couch surrounded by a group of black men
and women, with Mayor John Lindsay in the middle, smiling. He
was probably one of the only white people to ever come to our
apartment, besides my father. Lindsay, I would later learn, was a
Republican, but a socially liberal one. He was believed by many to
be a friend to black people, who was determined to see Harlem
thrive. The streets would be cleaned up, there would be jobs, he
would say when he campaigned uptown. Miriam raised money for
him, went door to door telling tired people why they should vote
for him. Many years later she told me that he was the last politician she ever believed in.

This was the beginning of Miriam's loss of faith in Harlem, of
the idea that things could change for the better, both for the neighborhood and for black people. After a time this loss would surface
as the deep disillusionment she would feel until the end of her life.
Malcolm X was assassinated just over a year before I was born,
Martin Luther King two years after. Miriam would tell me stories
about boycotting stores along 125th Street that wouldn't hire
black workers, and picketing in neighborhoods that were still seg-
regated. She described, with tears in her eyes, the March on Washington, how she stood near the great Reflecting Pool with the
hundreds of thousands of other hopeful, sweating, dreaming people, how she almost fainted when Dr. King began speaking. I don't
know if I witnessed her reaction to Dr. King's murder, if I saw the
news reports on television or heard people crying together in hud-
dles throughout our building and in the streets outside. I would
have been too young to understand the grief, the loss of faith that

she and so many others had felt on that day, too young to read in the television images of flames and shattered glass the frustration that burned in those broken years, in Harlem and in black neighborhoods all over the country.

I think for a long time Miriam dealt with this upheaval and loss by redirecting her energies; in the early 1970s she began working in housing development, supporting tenants on rent strike because their landlords ignored the legions of rats invading their buildings, fighting the city for new low-income apartments and rehabilitation of the blocks of burned-out, boarded-up buildings all over Harlem. She helped found an organization whose work was to preserve historical landmarks uptown. As a little girl, I remember smoky late-night meetings and strange people ringing our doorbell, days on end where I saw her only as she was leaving early in the morning, coming home too late for me to kiss her goodnight. Looking back now I understand the devotion of Miriam's activist years, and also the desperation. It's as though she were trying to keep her childhood image of Harlem alive, not, this time, because of its past glamour, but because of its dignity, and its people's dignity.

I see myself as a little girl walking down 125th Street with her—she's taken me along while she goes shopping or runs errands. She's wearing one of her theatrical hats and moving in her brisk, erect way, nose a little in the air. She seems to know everyone, greeting people every block it seems, introducing me, *my little granddaughter, my baby*. I can hardly keep track of the people we meet. Miriam points out different buildings to me, facades made of thick, rustic stones, doorways flanked by fluted columns, rows of gently arched windows like sighs. Miriam was a part of these buildings, these streets. They embraced her, sheltered her, and it seems that as she fought for them she was also fighting for her own life.

. . .

MY MOTHER was changing, too. For her, the world outside of Harlem was all motion and conversation, glitter and speed. Her job up at Columbia had allowed her to imagine other lives for herself than the one Miriam had chosen for her. This had nothing to do with the real or imagined ivy growing up the sides of the university buildings or the great, beckoning library on whose steps she would eat her lunch each day. Meeting my father was only the beginning; he must have seemed so sophisticated to her then, with his books on Eastern philosophy and his interest in foreign films. My father tells me that the strongest impression he has of her from when they were together was her determination to get out of Harlem. *It was an obsession with her,* he says, more than thirty years later. I think that as a young girl she had been waiting for some magic door to open; maybe she'd step through it and be back in California with her father; maybe it would lead her to Europe, where she had dreamed of going ever since she met her German exchange student boyfriend. Her few short years with my father, working at Columbia, were that magic door. Once she had gone across its threshold, she would never be the same.

After I was born and she and my father had split up, that period of my mother's life must have seemed like a barely remembered dream to her. I must have been around three years old when she found a new job as a waitress at a bar owned by a famous football player. She began meeting film directors and musicians, actresses and artists. One of my mother's friends was a white, blond stewardess, who lived in a tiny apartment in the Village. My mother would take me along to visit her; I remember the furniture was covered with multicolored cloth, mirrored and beaded. Incense was always burning in a corner; it tickled my nose and made me sneeze. There was also a woman named Tanya, long-legged and cocoa-skinned, who came from Georgia.

Tanya was one of the few black fashion models getting work in the mainstream press, although these jobs never came easily. She would become my mother's closest friend. Tanya would come by our apartment in the early evenings and she and my mother would get ready to go out to a party or a dinner at a fancy restaurant, each of them dressed in velvet and lace, painting their eyes with shimmering blue powder. To me they looked like butterflies, settled only for a moment before they took flight. Tanya helped my mother find her first modeling jobs, and later they would travel to Europe together for their first fashion show. It was the era of "Black is Beautiful," although this was interpreted quite differently in Harlem than it was at the white photographers' studios and the parties downtown where my mother now found herself.

My mother began getting more modeling work and even bit parts in films. She decided she would become a movie star. A film director she met told her she could be *a black Marilyn Monroe*. These were the terms that women like my mother and Tanya would have to accept, the cost of admission to get through the magic door. You could be a black this or a chocolate-covered that, a more colorful version of some original that had grown momentarily out of fashion. My mother went to casting calls and cattle calls, carrying her black leather portfolio with her. Each time she rang the bell at a photographer's studio or a casting agent's office, she had to leave her intellect behind. There was no room for it in this new life. This new world she found herself in, a white world, wanted black bodies, bodies that served, entertained, or gave pleasure. What place was there for my mother's ideas, her curiosity? What place was there for a black woman genius? These are my concerns, my childish desire to go back in time and shield my mother from what I believe was a world that could never appreciate her. She sees it all differently: *I had fun,* she says now, *people noticed me. I had beautiful clothes, met everyone. It was what I wanted.*

Maybe my disdain for the life she chose is not about protecting her at all. Maybe I'm just jealous, and have been since I was a small child. The parties, the admiration, the boyfriends, they took her away from me. I wanted her at home in our apartment in Harlem, believed that she, Miriam, and I could have made our own world. I didn't want to share either of them with anyone else. What I couldn't have imagined back then was that my mother wanted a life of her own. She was twenty-one years old with a three-year-old child. My father did so little to help; she had already worked for years to support us. I don't think Miriam realized that it was her own earlier life in L.A. that my mother was now emulating. My mother had learned about femininity and beauty from Miriam, just as she had learned to love books. My mother, who would sneak into Miriam's closet after she had gone out and slip her tiny feet into Miriam's stiletto shoes. My mother, who would carry the secret of her intelligence with her through the magic door.

At home in Harlem, Miriam still bragged about my mother's IQ, to anyone who would listen, but she stopped asking her about college. I would watch her cut out the pictures of my mother in newspapers and magazines. She would paste them into a scrapbook that she would take out whenever she had company: Here was her daughter modeling the latest maxi skirt, made of great blocks of colored fabric, like a designer quilt. Here she was in an Afro wig, wearing giant hoop earrings that dangled toward her shoulders. Miriam would keep this scrapbook for the rest of her life, in the back of her closet with all the documents of the life she had lived: birth certificates, journals scrawled in her long, twisting handwriting that I could never decipher, old photographs, letters kept neatly folded in their envelopes, almost as if they had never been read.

I WAS JUST about to start the first grade when I began to notice that Miriam and my mother were never home at the same time anymore. The three of us didn't sit together on the couch and watch television the way we used to, me sitting between them with my glass of milk and Nilla wafers on a napkin on my lap. I try to thread out from my memory images of them together from that time—I never realized how few there really are. Maybe their closeness was something I had only imagined from the beginning, maybe what was unraveling was a much more tenuous bond, an indefinite truce now suspended. For as long as I can remember, conversations between Miriam and my mother were strained when they happened at all, the words they exchanged always sounded clipped, their meanings seemed caught in an electric field of unexpressed emotion. Their forced politeness, which only hinted at the weight of all that remained unsaid between them, is the only clue I have of what life was like those last months before my mother finally left for good. I don't remember the day she moved out, only that at some point she found an apartment in the West Village, a studio in a brownstone, on a street lined with pear trees that blossomed white flowers in the spring. I don't remember if I cried as my mother packed her bags. I don't remember if I believed her when she told me that she'd send for me soon. I don't know what ever happened to the sheepskin coat; I never saw it after that.

CHAPTER FIVE

An image of me with my father: We're at the Museum of Modern Art. I'm around four, he's holding me up to a painting, pointing at the colors. My legs are dangling in the air, and I'm reaching out to touch the painting, which is protected by a layer of glass. It's Van Gogh's *Starry Night*. *Look at how he makes the stars out of these swishes of gold,* he says to me, and I want to crawl inside the painting, climb up that blue night sky to those golden swirls. There is no photograph of us together here, no witness to this scene. It's the first real memory I have of my father.

He likes to brag that I could tell a Cézanne from a Picasso by the time I was five years old. When I was in college I invited him to a screening of my first student film. He told this story, chest a little puffed out, his arm wrapped around my shoulder, to my teachers and friends; he seemed to bask in their studied wonder at my early precociousness. I wondered at the time if what he was really responding to was their approval of him as a parent. It's true, he had taken me to museums and taught me about painting and sculpture and photography, it was his gift to me. Maybe telling other people was his way of proving that he was really there when

I was growing up. A kind of absolution for the times when he was absent. Maybe these museum stories work in a similar way for me now—it hadn't been a dream, I did have a father, and he cared enough to teach me the difference between one modern artist and another.

In the summertime, my father used to come pick me up at Miriam's and take me to the Metropolitan Museum. On hot weekend days he and I would walk across Central Park from West Harlem to the Upper East Side. The entrance to the park was down the block from Miriam's apartment—just inside, there was a public pool where my mother would take me on hot mornings. A familiar sound from my childhood—the high, shrieking laughter of children splashing in water. A sound of resilience and expectation, it spilled out over the edges of the low stone wall that marked the park's border, washed over the relentless concrete sidewalks and scorched asphalt streets on the other side. My father would walk me past the pool, past the lake where old women fed ducks and boys tried to catch the small, flat fish that darted through the cloudy water. These were uncomplicated moments with my father, above us the endless green of the trees, the *whish*ing sound of the leaves caught by a rare breeze, my small yellow hand in his thick olive one. I didn't know the extent of the bitterness that raged between my mother, Miriam, and him over his responsibilities as a parent, didn't know of the battles he had with his own parents over me. On days like this I would forget all the times I had waited for him and he didn't show up.

The Met was a world unto itself: rooms of immense stone Buddhas and eloquent African masks unfolded into rooms lined with paintings of faraway landscapes and ships on stormy seas; corridors of ancient gold jewelry in glass cases opened out onto airy halls with fountains gurgling at their centers. My father would always want to go to the Egyptian rooms first, but I would tug his arm toward the medieval wing, where the knights in armor waited on their silent horses. The arms and armor collection was in a bright hall past the dim stone rooms of the medieval wing. Great banners hung overhead in red and gold, appliquéd with griffins, crowns, ancient family crests. Against the walls, whole suits of armor stood enclosed in glass and surrounded by the paraphernalia of medieval warfare—shields painted with fleurs-de-lis, lances with hooked blades, gleaming swords. In the center of the room, on a low platform, were four equestrian knights carrying raised lances, their horses fully armored and poised in midgallop. The knights wore steel suits of armor, inlaid with gold and decorated with intricate patterns—leaves and flowers, musical instruments, mythological figures. Light poured in from wide, sloping windows just below the ceiling, making the whole space feel as if it were floating on air.

I could stay in that room for hours. I was mesmerized by the stillness of it, the hushed voices of the other people around us, whispering as if in reverence of the kings and dukes for whom the armor was made so long ago. The knights on their horses seemed to have been frozen in time, caught just as they were about to charge off to some distant battle. I would stand directly in front of them, eyes closed, imagining that at any moment they would come to life. The horses would leap snorting and whinnying off the platform, the knights' armor would crash and clang as they flew past me, there would be thunderous galloping and horns blowing. All the glass cases would shatter. *Hey, where did you go off to?* my father would say, nudging me and pulling me out of my reverie. I never shared these fantasies with him—I think I was embarrassed by the violence of my imagination, vaguely aware as only a child can be of breaking the rules. Was a girl supposed to be thinking of such things? Was a little black girl from Harlem, who wore pigtails tied with bright pink ribbons, meant to dream of galloping horses and clashing swords? Two of the suits of armor were Italian—each time we came, as if for the first time, my father would point this out to me. He'd tell me how much more beautiful the Italian armor was than the rest, how much more intricate in detail and sleek in design. I always agreed, eager to please him, eager, I think now, to show that I belonged. *Yay Italy,* he would say, raising his fist in triumph. *Yay Italy,* I would shout back.

This is one of the earliest acknowledgments I can remember of my Italian American identity, my *italianità*. It was something my father encouraged from the beginning, a claiming of me in terms of our shared ethnicity, our common connection to a faraway land that seemed to me out of a fairy tale, a place that existed once upon a time. The other points of identification I had with Italy—also in the realm of myth and fairy tale—were given to me by Miriam. There was my "Roman nose," of course. And there was the time that Miriam brought home a small plaster copy of the *Venus de Milo*— the kind that might sit in a garden—and set it up on a marble pedestal in the living room. *It's broken,* I said as she took it from one corner of the room to the other, trying to decide where it fit best. *Maybe the arms fell off at the store.* She gave me an exasperated look. *That's the way it's supposed to be. It's classical art, and it's part of your heritage.* She was so pleased that she'd been able to find this Venus on sale—she saw it as the crowning glory of the apartment. Every week, she would polish the ghostly white face, the rigid, pointed breasts, the half-hidden feet, and turn the statue from one barely perceptible angle to another so it would catch the light better.

Sometimes before I went to sleep Miriam would read to me from her book of Greek mythology—fantastic stories of wrathful gods and beautiful goddesses, humans changed into birds and trees, wild, living landscapes and talking oracles. I loved the slow, even rhythm of her voice when she read, the way I was carried along on its honeyed current and transported out of my small self into worlds I loved to imagine. The myth she read most often, and the one that I grew to request above all others, was that of Persephone, the maiden of spring, and her mother, the grain goddess Demeter. I would be perfectly still as she opened the book, listening to the incantatory sounds of her breath and the pages turning. Miriam would remind me again and again that the myth took place in Sicily, long, long ago: *This is your story, this is where your father's people come from.* I understood that it was necessary to remember this, although I wasn't sure why. It seemed like another one of those things that I would need when I was older, the way the Pittsburgh aunts told me I would need my "fine" features.

Miriam would recount how Persephone was innocently picking flowers by the side of a lake with her friends when she was abducted by Hades, god of the underworld, to be his bride. She cried out as he drove her in his black chariot down, down into the center of the earth, but no one came to help her. When Demeter heard the news, she raged for nine days and nine nights, mourning her daughter as lost forever. In her grief, she caused a drought to destroy the crops of the fields, vineyards, and orchards. The land lay fallow, humans and animals starved. The other gods and goddesses begged Demeter to make food grow again in the parched soil, on the withered vines and the trees' empty branches, but she was inconsolable. Zeus, Persephone's own father, who had allowed Hades to take her in the first place, finally intervened. He made a deal with both husband and mother, that Persephone would divide her time between them both. During the spring and summer, Demeter and her daughter are reunited and everything flourishes on earth. In winter, Persephone descends into the underworld, where she is queen of the dead. Demeter is bereft once more, and the earth is barren until her daughter returns.

As I grew older, long after the age of bedtime stories, I began to respond almost instinctively to this myth—as if I were growing into it. Not because of its origin in a distant place to which I was somehow connected, but because I saw myself in the figure of Persephone, the good girl destined to live a life split in two. A girl who is always leaving, whose every homecoming is a goodbye. It was many years before I understood the irony that it was my African American grandmother who gave me this Greek/Sicilian myth, who encouraged me to claim it as my own. I don't know if my Italian grandmother Gilda knew the story—if she did, she never repeated it. Was it lost when her own mother, Luisa, left the Old World behind and landed in Italian Harlem, the old stories too heavy a weight to carry into the future? Or would Luisa have held the myth close, like a memory of home, passing it on to Gilda in their tenement apartment while she cooked and scrubbed and sewed for her growing family? Luisa could not read or write in English or Italian—Gilda had had some years of school, but was not encouraged to read. Always too much to do, too much work, too many mouths to feed. In their world, what kind of woman would dare steal time for herself, dare to pick up a book or a pen? Somehow Miriam had dared for them, for herself, for me. A black woman with a high school education and a desperate love of books, she found a way to put the story of Persephone and Demeter, an ancient story of the troubled ties between mothers and daughters, into my hands. She claimed it for all of us.

I think Miriam's emphasis on my European heritage sprang from her struggle to make sense of her own complicated identity. Her family had been in the industrial North for four generations. She grew up in a neighborhood and a family where African American and European immigrant cultures coexisted, indeed bled into each other. She made bratwurst along with her black-eyed peas and cornbread, and said *gesundheit!* when anybody sneezed. Anything African or afrocentric was foreign and slightly embarrassing to her. There were no symbols of black power in Miriam's apartment—like many of her generation, she blamed black militants for the drugs and crime that afflicted Harlem in the 1960s and '70s, for young people's loss of respect for their elders, and worst of all, for what she saw as a sudden and overwhelming rejection of education. There were no African masks bought from vendors on 125th Street, no kente cloth folded into regal headwraps for special occasions.

At Miriam's high school, she was taught Western Civilization—the perfection and magnanimity of the classical world, of Shakespeare, the Renaissance, the Enlightenment. She was taught that African slaves had been brought out of savagery and eternal damnation by their white masters, who had kindly shared with them their great civilization. Yet at that same high school, Miriam had refused to stand for the Pledge of Allegiance after she had seen photographs of a Southern lynching in the *Pittsburgh Courier,* the city's black newspaper. It was the first time she had seen such an image, a black man strung up in a tree, his head hanging to one side like a discarded rag doll, his face a holocaust of gashes and welts. Day after day Miriam sat while the rest of the class saluted the American flag, until her parents were called in and she was convinced that such a thing wasn't worth being expelled over. *Change is coming,* Momma had assured her, *just you wait and see.*

My black inheritance: defiant, desired, conflicted, provisional. My Italian inheritance: a mythic landscape and a family I barely knew. Yet on those childhood afternoons in the armory room of the Met with my father, I wouldn't have been conscious of the uncertainties of blood and culture, race and color. At five, six, eight years old, all I really wanted was to be a knight. I wanted to feel the weight and heat of metal against my body and to hear it clatter as I moved, to close the visor of a great, plumed helmet over my face. I had never been interested in blank-faced Barbies with their townhouses and stewardess outfits, or fat, staring baby dolls that you had to push around in a stroller. I often longed to be a princess in the fairy tales I read, to live happily ever after with a prince in a castle, but when I stood before those shining knights on their fearless horses, I was enchanted by their power. Silent, covered in steel from head to toe, they seemed invulnerable. I longed to be that strong, that safe, that untouchable.

Armor was skin that protected you from harm. It could not be penetrated. It hid you from recognition, from judgment. My skin only caused trouble—it was always too light or too dark, always a problem. Once I was taken out of my first-grade class by a social worker who wanted to know if I was being beaten at home. I bruised easily. I was clumsy and fell down a lot, thrashed in my sleep. My arms and legs were often covered with black and blue blotches that spread like a stigmata just underneath the surface of my skin. The bruises took weeks to fade, and people noticed. After a riot of accusations between my mother, Miriam, and my father, I was taken to a clinic, where a doctor gave me a blood test. It turned out that I had the gene for beta-thalassemia, or Mediterranean anemia. A type of anemia common among southern Italians. All over Harlem there were children who suffered from sickle-cell anemia, a "black people's disease." But my red blood cells took a different shape. From the beginning I was marked, deep within my body and also on its surface: different. I decided that I would grow myself a skin of armor, only mine would be hidden on the inside. It would be made of blazing gold and silver, engraved with fire-breathing dragons and roaring lions. No one would know when I was wearing it, but whenever I had it on, nothing would be able to hurt me.

THE COVER OF *Life* magazine from the day I was born shows fighter planes streaking across a lurid yellow and green sky. The caption reads: *Special Section on Vietnam—A Searching Assessment.* My father had received his draft notice sometime just before or just after my birth. His memory of this period has shifted over the years—at one time, he told me he got the notice while my mother was pregnant; later he said that I was a few months old already. Either way, because my parents weren't married, my father wasn't exempted from duty. He cooperated and enlisted, thinking that he might forestall the inevitability that he would be sent to the front lines in Vietnam. Maybe he would be made an officer, he reasoned, and be needed for some kind of special operations on a base in the States. My father says this, laughing a little, as if it were a scam he was pulling on the U.S. Army, as if he really believed he could have outsmarted them. He went to a camp at a location he still won't disclose, where he signed up for training in guided missiles, *knowing that they didn't use nuclear weapons over in Vietnam, so there would be no need for my trade.* He trained at the base for a year and a half, was promoted to corporal. I don't know what the relationship was between him and my mother by then—both tell me they don't remember.

There is a deep silence around the moment of my birth, an empty space where my father is supposed to be. No one remembers when my father saw me for the first time. There are no photographs of him holding me as a baby wrapped in pink blankets, none of me hobbling over to him as a toddler, his arms outstretched to catch me if I fell. He doesn't seem disturbed by this fact—like my mother, he says simply, *It was a long time ago.* My mother says he would come up to Harlem when he was on leave, bringing a little money for food, staying for a couple of hours to play games with me. I picture the three of us in the living room on a warm afternoon, the sun streaming through the windows. My father is bouncing me on his lap, I'm laughing and gurgling up at him. I probably don't understand who he is—*dada* is not among my first words. My mother sits on the other side of the room, watching, impatient for the visit to be over. It's possible that just before this moment they had a huge fight, my mother raging against my father for not coming to see me more often, for not helping more. My father would have cringed a little, as he has always done when confronted, made vague excuses, vague promises to do better. Or maybe by this time my mother is resigned to his evasions, just lets him play with me: *Who is daddy's girl, huh? Who's daddy's little baby?*

My father would spend the rest of his leave time with his family up in the Bronx. I have a photograph of him with my cousins Mike and Marie in front of my Aunt Angela's building. My father is wearing a khaki-colored army uniform, a green brimmed cap perched on his head. He's kneeling down—one arm around Marie, one arm around Mike, hugging them close. Marie must be around four—she's four years older than I am, so I must have been just a baby when the picture was taken. She's wearing a short pink coat with a matching hat and scarf, white patent-leather shoes, and white ankle socks. Her bare, plump legs are the same pale pink as her clothes. Mike is ten, skinny and angular, with a bashful smile. His black suit, with a white carnation in the lapel, seems out of place, as though he were on his way to a funeral. My father is clean-shaven—the last time he would ever be without a cover of facial hair. I've had this picture for years, though I'm not sure now who gave it to me. One thing I never noticed before—my father is grasping Marie's and Mike's hands as he holds them, his large dark hands covering their small white ones. I don't know what is more significant—the fact of his darkness, that of his immigrant peasant father, against the children's lightness—or the intimate, almost urgent way that my father has gathered them around him. As if he were trying to protect them from some impending danger.

My father was sent to Vietnam in 1967. He was part of an infantry unit that patrolled the jungle and the outskirts of nearby villages. His job was to cook the meals for the men in his platoon, breakfast, lunch, and dinner every day for a year. The guided-missile job had somehow fallen through—my father says he thought he would be learning skills, getting an education in electronics, but he was assigned most of the grunt work—painting missiles, greasing them, pushing them onto racks for storage. With his Bronx accent and his Italian last name, he didn't fit in with the other soldiers in his group, the pale New England boys from famous colleges and good families. They were given the more challenging jobs—the secret, important work of planning the total destruction of other people. My father would not see any of them on the front lines.

He decided to volunteer for kitchen duty instead. His grandmother Luisa had taught him to cook in her kitchen in East Harlem when he was a child. He had been different from the other neighborhood boys, who at nine and ten years old already smoked cigarettes and shot craps, ran errands for wise guys. My father watched as his brother, his cousins, and his friends got into gang fights with other boys because they lived on a different block, or because their parents came from Naples and not Sicily or Calabria, or because they spoke Spanish, or because their skin was brown. Luisa recognized something tender and unguarded in him, kept him close to her. My father, the quiet one, the baby of the family, Luisa's favorite. I see him at seven years old, standing at the stove on a wooden chair, stirring great pots of sauce, thick and red as blood. Luisa holds him steady, whispers stories in his ear about the small stone village where she was born. How she would wander through the surrounding woods, picking wild mushrooms and chestnuts. The chestnuts had saved her family many times from starvation, ground into flour for bread, roasted whole, or chopped into thin soups when there was no hope of meat. While the other boys were learning the language of the street, of territory and muscle and hard luck, Luisa taught my father the language of olive oil, tomatoes, and garlic, of honey, water, and flour. She taught him the arts of sustenance and survival. These he took with him to the war.

In the makeshift camps the platoon constructed and broke down every few days, moving from place to place as orders were given them, my father would set up his own small kitchen. He hauled cartons of canned and powdered food from site to site, carried stashes of dried herbs and spices in the pockets of his fatigues, and cooked over a gasoline stove. He made pots of beef stew and bean soups and spaghetti with meatballs—*That was their favorite,* he says now with a smile—as streams of mortar and rocket fire flared and sputtered not far in the distance. Because his skills were so necessary for the survival of his unit, he was spared from actively participating in combat. Instead, he saw many of his friends shot to death or blown up by grenades, images of carnage he won't describe for me. He says only, *It was pretty bad.* Even as a cook, though, he wasn't completely safe from danger. He's told me stories of being attacked by rats and shot at by snipers as he lit the stove in the dark early mornings, of having to go out by helicopter to the more remote places his platoon mates patrolled, and dropping containers of food down to them while the helicopter was fired on by unseen enemy soldiers. It's the sound of the helicopter that he remembers most, the endless hacking of the blades in the air. Even now he hears it in his dreams.

He was twenty-two years old. His platoon mates—all working class, many black and Latino—were the same age or younger. My father tells me that at first he believed the war was just, that communism was a danger to the entire world and had to be stopped. He had grown up during the duck-and-cover campaigns of the 1950s, he and his classmates huddling under their desks during test drills in the event of nuclear war with the Soviet Union. He thought the Vietnamese people wanted the Americans' help, his help. Only after a while he couldn't tell who the enemy was anymore. He had seen the bodies of women, old men, little children lying along roads, in ditches, at the edges of villages. He knew black and Latino soldiers who talked about deserting, refusing to be used as cannon fodder for the White Man. And then there were some white soldiers who just wanted to kill as many "gooks" as possible, maybe win a Purple Heart and come home as heroes.

My father listened to their talk and decided that the only thing that mattered to him was to survive. If he could make it another day there, he would be one day closer to home. In the meantime, he found a way to numb the wild fear that snapped constantly at his back. He doesn't remember the day he first tried heroin, or who gave it to him. The days flowed one into the other under those napalm skies, the nights he spent sleeping in trenches dug into the wet earth were as one long, dark night. In the beginning he snorted the drug, feeling the warm rush seep into his brain. It filled up the empty space behind his eyes where the tears had been. Later he shot it into his veins, the needle passing from one soldier to another, blood into blood. And together they floated on a dream-cloud high, suspended between life and death.

CHAPTER SIX

My father was born in East Harlem during World War II, a miracle baby. At a time when so many young men from the neighborhood were being killed on faraway battlefields, the birth of a boy was something special. When Gilda came home from the hospital, her neighbors threw her a victory party. I imagine people wandering in and out of the apartment all day and long into the night, bringing gifts and blessings for her and her new son. An American flag and an Italian flag hanging over her bed, just above the wooden crucifix that guarded her while she slept. It was 1944—Italy had just fallen to the Allies—and Italian American soldiers were fighting their way across the country. For many of them, it would be their first encounter with the *paese* of their parents, their grandparents. The longed-for homeland, now enemy territory. Gilda had not supported Mussolini, although Luigi praised him gruffly for making the trains run on time. She had not sent Il Duce her gold wedding band as had some of the women she knew from the neighborhood. Her own three brothers were fighting overseas in the American army, and Gilda must have felt that she had to choose sides. I remember a picture that she kept on her dresser in New Jersey: two of her brothers—I'm not sure which—standing arm in arm in front of a shop in East Harlem. It was taken just before they left to fly bombing missions in the Pacific. They were so handsome in their crisply pressed officer's uniforms, blue-eyed and smiling bravely.

Gilda's other son and daughter had been born more than a decade before. She was only twenty-eight when my father was born, but she must have believed that her childbearing years were behind her. Her relationship with her husband had been difficult from the beginning—it had long grown cold by the time my father was born, a dead weight propped up by the daily and incontestable responsibilities of family and community. Luigi was a drinker, loud and violent, although no one in our family has ever used the word "alcoholic" to describe him. During the days he worked as a laborer, bricklaying mostly, although I've heard that he once laid track for the Third Avenue El. At night he tended bar at a neighborhood saloon. There were other women, many of them. Gilda worked all day as a chambermaid in the Gramercy Park Hotel; when she came home she cooked for the children, cleaned the small apartment, helped them with their homework as best she could. I never heard her mention any girlfriends from this time of her life—it seems her only companions were her mother, who lived next door, and her three brothers and their wives. Sometimes my father jokes that Gilda was so lonely she had had an affair with the milkman, and that maybe he's not his father's son after all. *My mom was pretty good-looking in those days,* he says, *and my dad was such a prick.*

When he was nine months old, my father had almost died of whooping cough. He had to have an operation on his lung—a long, jagged scar under his right shoulder blade marks the spot where the surgeon opened him up. Even after he came home from the hospital, it was still not certain whether he would live or die. Luisa had been known as a root woman throughout the neighborhood, a craft she had learned from her own mother. She knew the medicinal—and the magical—properties of many different kinds of plants: asphodel to ward off impotence, mallow to relieve toothache, chamomile to calm frayed nerves and upset stomachs. These she grew in pots on her fire escape. Other herbs she kept dried in paper bags in her closet, the secret herbs that she used to help women—bundled as charms to keep men from straying, packed into poultices to relieve a black eye, steeped into potent teas to ease labor pains or to end unwanted pregnancies.

My father remembers that whenever he had a headache, Luisa would drip olive oil into a bowl of water to see if he had been struck by *il malocchio,* the evil eye. When I was a child, she had given me a small gold horn on a delicate chain to protect me from the same danger. I wore it, the one gift Luisa had given me, around my neck for many years afterward, until I lost it one day at the beach. I had been floating on my back in the water when I noticed it was gone. Again and again I dove under the waves, searching the sandy bottom for a glint of gold, but the water was cloudy, and its sharp saltiness stung my eyes.

Luisa's magic couldn't help my father, nor could the magic of the doctors. So she and Gilda prayed to Saint Anthony, the healer of sick children and patron of lost causes. They built a shrine near my father's crib, a statue of the saint the size of a small child, surrounded by flowers. Each night they kept a vigil there, kneeling before Saint Anthony on the bare wooden floor until their knees ached. The saint gazed down on them, his pitying smile a reassurance that he understood their sorrow. In one arm he held a lily, in the other the baby Jesus—soft-featured and sad-eyed, almost maternal, he was a saint women could trust with the lives of their children. Votive candles flickered all over the darkened apartment—the musky smoke rose with Gilda and Luisa's prayers: *O holy Saint Anthony, gentlest of Saints, miracles wait on your word.* Neighbors came with great loaves of braided bread and steaming pots of soup, and letters filled with prayers dictated by relatives in Calabria, Toronto, Argentina, who couldn't read or write. My father survived, and the women rejoiced.

My father was too young to remember any of this, but he grew up hearing the legend of his wondrous recovery. Every birthday, Luisa would tearfully recount how he had been snatched from the arms of death, *u mortu.* Gilda would bark the story at him as she bundled him up for school on winter mornings, yanking his hat down around his ears, knotting his scarf close against his neck, warning him to stay inside and not exert himself.

My father spent his childhood learning that he was special, fragile, that the expectations his mother and grandmother held for his older, heartier siblings did not apply to him. His own body confirmed this—he was small and thin, tired easily. Quiet and sensitive, he was kept from doing heavy chores around the house, and shielded from the fights that were escalating between his parents.

THE 1920 census records my father's family as living on East 113th Street. I've heard many stories about the building they lived in, or fragments of stories, pieced together from my father's distant childhood recollections and from Gilda's fading memory as an old woman. Gilda began suffering from the symptoms of Alzheimer's disease in her early eighties. The first thing that happened was a blurring of the past into the present. When she spoke, the years would flow into each other like the mingling of tides when a river meets the sea. We would sit together at her kitchen table in New

Jersey, and she'd gaze out the window, squinting her eyes and craning her neck, as if she were searching for something in the backyard. *I wish I was in Harlem again,* she'd sigh. *Everyone was so nice there—not like here. They're still waiting for me to come home.* I realized that what she was trying to find outside her window were the familiar faces of the tenement buildings that lined 113th Street. Covered with black soot, laundry hanging from the fire escapes, this was the landscape of her youth. *I can't see it anymore,* she'd murmur, shaking her head.

The mythology of East Harlem, Italian Harlem: it was safe, it was clean, it was "our" place, the family was together, everybody looked out for each other, so safe you didn't even have to lock your door. This is the first thing my father will say if you ask him about East Harlem—the doors to all the apartments in their building were always open. Blood relatives, *cumpari* and *cummari,* neighbors and friends would constantly flow into each other's homes, visiting for a cup of coffee; commiserating over a wayward husband, a willful daughter, a son falling in with "the wrong people"; sharing news from the Other Side, who got married and who died in the village back home, who just arrived and was looking for work or a place to stay. In the evenings, Gilda would send my father to buy wine from a man down the hall who made his own, fermenting the grapes in jugs in the basement. On feast days, the women would crowd into each other's kitchens to make fresh pasta, laying thick stands of *ferrazzuoli* over the backs of chairs to dry.

If I'm not careful, I can easily succumb to the seduction of these images of intimacy. *We never used to have to lock our doors, before,* my father says. I devour these words of safety, gorge myself in this fantasy of total community, total belonging. Imagine a place for myself in these rooms with their open doors. The shame of this: my memories of fear are inseparable from my sense of home, of community in black Harlem. The padlocks and bar locks on the all the doors, Miriam peering suspiciously out the peephole whenever someone rang the doorbell, the constant worries among the neighbors about strangers getting into the lobby through the broken front door. So that even my memories are a betrayal. Because what I feel whenever my father talks about the open doors of his childhood is not righteous anger—at the conditions that created those dangers that preyed on black Harlem—but the indignant envy of a child: why did he get to have that life and I didn't?

So I have to break the spell, refuse the seduction. Because my Italian family's conviction that they were safe, that East Harlem was their own perfect little world, could only exist with the exclusion of those deemed outsiders. When Puerto Rican immigrants began to move into the area, in the 1930s and '40s, Italian landlords refused to rent them apartments. Italian American gangs patrolled the streets, chasing away with baseball bats any Latinos who dared to cross Third Avenue. My Uncle Tony once told me how when he was a student at Benjamin Franklin High School, a race riot broke out because African American students were being bused in from the other side of Harlem. The fighting went on for days. *We only brought our bats because they already had knives,* Uncle Tony said. Finally, the progressive neighborhood politician Vito Marcantonio invited Frank Sinatra and Paul Robeson to come address the students and try to broker a truce.

My grandparents and their three children finally moved away from East Harlem in the early 1950s. My grandfather's two brothers had moved to the Bronx a few years earlier, taking advantage of the postwar economic upswing to open a tailor shop near Westchester Square. Using money from bank loans that were readily available to white people who wanted to leave the ethnic ghettos of Manhattan, my great-uncles had bought a two-family house and had settled in with their wives and children. Gilda and Luigi, my father, and his brother and sister were still living in a building on 113th Street between Second and Third Avenues when they heard the news that the city was planning to raze the old tenements on their block and build a series of low-income apartment towers in their place. It was something that many Italian Americans in the neighborhood had fought for, especially the women, who had marched in the streets with placards demanding better housing. My father remembers Gilda reading the eviction notice that had been slipped under their door. *We didn't want to leave,* he tells me now, *but we had no choice.* Luigi found a cheap apartment near his brothers' store in the Bronx, and got a job as a bartender in a bar just under the elevated train on Westchester Square. When the buildings went up on 113th Street and working class black families began moving into them, large numbers of Italian Americans fled the neighborhood rather than live in integrated housing. *They didn't build those buildings for us,* my Uncle Tony says. *We were betrayed.*

IF I READ between the lines, the census record from 1920 becomes a map that leads me back through the scraps of story, inherited and overheard, that make up my father's family history— my history. The record describes two conjoined households in one apartment: The Yacino family—I've also seen it spelled Iacino or Jacino: Luisa's father, Pasquale; her mother, Carmella; and her brothers, Rocco and Vincenzo—and the Mancuso family: Luisa's husband, Salvatore, and four children: Gilda, Joe, Michael and Elvira. Luisa is listed under her parents' name as "daughter"; Salvatore, "son-in-law"; and the children are represented almost as a separate clan. Gilda was Luisa's first child—she had been born in the apartment seven years earlier. Elvira, one of two daughters who did not live past childhood, was two years old. I don't know how much longer she would live, or if the other daughter, whose name is now lost, had already died or had yet to be born. The youngest son, Frank, probably arrived shortly after the census was taken. Luisa was twenty-eight.

Gilda grew up in this tangle of family—three generations, two languages, the living and the dying all together in a few small rooms. She slept in a fold-out bed in the living room with her siblings, spent most of the time that she wasn't at school helping her mother around the house. Luisa took in piecework to supplement the small and inconsistent income Salvatore brought in as a shoeshine man. Gilda would sit with Luisa in the kitchen, their heavy wooden table piled high with blouses or dresses on which they would sew fabric flowers and decorative buttons. I think of the famous photograph of the Italian immigrant woman with a towering bundle of clothes on her head, walking down a New York street. She's picked up her piecework from the factory, is carrying it home to finish it. It was long, painstaking work, done in the free moments between house- hold chores, after school and homework, in the evenings after din- ner had been cooked and the dishes washed. Gilda first told me about the piecework one day when she was sewing embroidered borders on my dungarees—I must have been around ten or eleven, outgrowing my clothes with alarming speed. She would buy the borders, embellished with brightly colored flowers, in a fabric store, and attach them whenever my pants got too short. *I used to do this every day when I was a little girl like you,* she said, pulling a strand of red thread through a long, thin needle. *But I had to sew other people's things that I didn't even know.* I wonder what it must have been like, the pretty flowers that felt like silk, the shiny buttons and velvet ribbons spread before her as she worked late into the night, decorating clothes that she would never get to wear.

As a girl, Gilda learned from her mother how to keep a spotless home, how to care for her younger siblings, how to feed a growing family, all preparation for the time when she would have a husband and children of her own. Luisa's cooking was legendary in the family: *The best food we ever had came from her hands* is the refrain that I heard again and again from my father, my Aunt Angela, and my Uncle Tony. They would often joke affectionately that Gilda didn't inherit her mother's skills in the kitchen. My father has also said that she *wasn't the brightest bulb in the box.* This seemed to be accepted family knowledge: she wasn't very smart, wasn't very strong, didn't measure up to her mother or the other women in the family as a cook, a wife, a mother. I never understood this collective disparagement—what I saw of her was a woman who spent her time deeply concentrated on the daily tasks of taking care of her family. My father still dreams of Luisa's extraordinary holiday feasts, dinners that lasted for hours, course upon course, her grown children and their children all pressed together around a table covered with white lace. But it is Gilda's simple, fortifying meals that I remember and long for, the Monday night lentil soup, the vinegary iceberg lettuce salads, the chicken wings baked with oregano, the salty tomato sauce whose memory lingers in my taste buds—the dull, hungry ache of nostalgia always on my tongue.

Gilda, the first one born in America—at home she was surrounded by the immigrant world of her parents and grandparents: an ancient dialect, a mother's magic that she never learned, traditions that taught her to be quiet and obedient, that her value as a female came from the labor of her hands and her body. At school, she spoke English, learned about the world outside East Harlem. She was the first person in her family to learn to read and write. Later, when she worked cleaning rooms at the Gramercy Park Hotel, she made more money than her aging father. Gilda the golden one, who carried her Old World, fairy-tale name with her on the downtown train like a crown too heavy for her head, who put on a black uniform and cleaned the soiled sheets of people who had the freedom to come and go as they pleased. Every week, she handed her wages over, first to her mother, and then, after she was married, to her husband. I wonder if she ever kept some of the money for herself, bought a dress adorned with real silk flowers, or sneaked off to a movie once in a while after work. Did she talk about her life with the other women who worked as maids at the hotel?

Most of what I know about Gilda's life begins when she was sixteen. It was the year she was married to my grandfather, Luigi. The story of the marriage has come to me only in pieces—secondhand information that my father and his siblings gleaned from their parents' arguments, and from whispered conversations among their aunts and uncles, overheard at the dinner table, in the hallways, on the stoop. The marriage had been arranged by Luisa—her daughter would be joined to a man from the village back home. A deal made between two families, a custom in southern Italy that was imported to Italian Harlem.

There are two opposing tales of my grandfather's arrival in America: In the first scenario, he came alone as a young man, the first of three brothers to make the journey from Calabria. He had lived in East Harlem for a number of years, working as a day laborer, when Luisa chose him for a son-in-law. In the second, he was the youngest of the brothers, who were already in East Harlem. He was the one still living in the village, and the marriage was arranged between Luisa and his family as a kind of sponsorship for him to come to New York. During the rare times when my father and Aunt Angela and Uncle Tony got together as adults—Uncle Tony had moved to Las Vegas when I was a child—they would argue about which story was true. I would sit with them at the dinner table as a teenager, listening to their rich, gravelly Bronx accents: Angela with her can of Pepsi and her pack of Parliament cigarettes in front of her, Tony drinking a beer, my father peeling an orange, dividing it up in segments for each of us.

Their father's immigration documents had been lost long ago—the "official" story did not exist. *Daddy was here first—I don't care what any of you says,* Angela would begin, taking a deep drag from her cigarette and blowing the smoke in a stream out of the side of her mouth. Tony would counter, *That's not what he told me— I was the only one that ever asked him.* They would end up joking that Luigi was always too drunk to get a straight answer out of him— the three of them, with their father's dark olive skin and full lips, giggling like naughty children. My father would turn to me and say, *All I know is that he was born in 1901.*

Gilda was in the tenth grade when the marriage was arranged. Once the date was set for the wedding, her parents took her out of school. Here again is a great silence. She never spoke of that time in her life, how it felt to have her parents tell her one day that she would be married within the year, that she didn't need any more school, she had already had more than enough. Education was wasted on girls, who would just grow up to be wives and mothers anyway—a belief Gilda's mother shared with her father. Like other girls in the neighborhood, the first generation born in Harlem, Gilda had gone to high school a few blocks from home. Many of her female classmates would graduate at eighteen and marry after that; a handful would even go to college. I don't know if Gilda ever imagined such a possibility for herself, if she ever truly believed her life held other options than that which was presented to her at sixteen. Her girlhood was over—she said goodbye to her textbooks and her notebooks and her pencils and prepared to become a wife.

KYM RAGUSA

I try to picture the day she and Luigi met, the same day, as the story goes, that their engagement was made official. It was a late afternoon, I imagine. Gilda is standing before the only mirror in the house, the one over the heavy oak bureau in her parents' bedroom. She's brushing her wavy, ink-black hair, pinching her cheeks to give them color. Luisa has been preparing for days, polishing the furniture, waxing the floors, cooking dishes that my father would remember later as only eaten on the most important occasions, like the rich sausage made from pig's blood that he called *a' sanguinaccia.* She's put out her best *biancheria,* the embroidered white linens that had been part of her dowry as a young bride, handmade by her own mother: lacy antimacassars for the couch and chairs, crisp, perfectly folded napkins, and a long tablecloth appliquéd with hearts and lovebirds that she's saved just for this moment.

This is a seduction of the highest order, a mother's seduction. The gleaming home, the intoxicating smells coming from the kitchen, and finally the beautiful daughter. Luigi comes to the Yacino apartment, bearing gifts for the family, a small token for Gilda—maybe a bouquet of flowers. The family assembles with much ceremony in the living room. Gilda sits silently across from her husband-to-be, wearing her best dress, eyes chastely downcast. Luisa makes the introduction, gesturing for the young couple to shake hands. Salvatore pours wine in the delicate glasses decorated with thin bands of gold that Gilda will one day inherit. Luigi is unusually reserved, shows little sign of the strident, angry man he will become. This is a good deal from his perspective, a wife to take care of him, a large family already settled and well connected in the neighborhood ready to embrace him as one of their own. Later the whole family sits down to an opulent celebratory dinner. Between courses, Gilda steals appraising glances at Luigi—what kind of husband will he be? Will he love her? Her parents and other relatives crowd around the new couple for a toast, wishing them a long life and *tante figghi maschi*—many sons.

It must have seemed like a dream to Gilda—watching Luisa sign away the rest of my teenage grandmother's life to a greenhorn she didn't know, who was ten years older and spoke no English. Did she find him handsome in his only suit, cleaned and pressed especially for this occasion, or was she frightened by his dark, intense eyes and his stiff, courtly manners? How much am I, the third-generation American granddaughter, reading into her story? What I know of her later life with my grandfather makes it difficult to imagine her before her troubles began, to imagine her as anything but a girl forced to grow up too soon. The wedding took place in 1930 at Our Lady of Mount Carmel, the church to which my family had been devoted since Luisa's arrival in East Harlem. Luisa went to mass there each morning, from the time she was a teenager until the day she died; Gilda and her siblings were baptized there, as were my father and his sister and brother. Gilda's was the first marriage among Luisa's children at Mount Carmel, imbuing the union with a particular gravitas. She was the first to take the vow to love, honor, and obey before the figure of the Madonna, magnificent in a gilded robe and a jeweled crown, who stood watch in a niche above the altar. I imagine Gilda on her knees in front of the priest, who performs the rites in Italian. Gilda is completely veiled, her hands pressed together in prayer. She gazes through the white lace at the face of the Madonna, hoping for some sign that she will be happy with the man kneeling next to her. Happily ever after. But there is no sign, and the Madonna remains inscrutable as an ancient pagan goddess.

An odd bit of amnesia that my father and I share: neither of us has any memory of ever seeing photographs from Gilda and Luigi's wedding. A formal shot must have been taken—Gilda wearing a white silk dress, Luigi in a new black suit—an intimate yet public recognition of the moment of their union. But my father can't remember seeing any among the other framed photographs in the apartments where he grew up. *There must have been a picture somewhere,* he says, trying to dredge up an image from the haze of his memory, *but it's like there's a veil over it.* And when I think back on the pictures I remember from the house in New Jersey—fading, slightly orange-tinted school portraits of my cousins and me at various ages; a snapshot of Lady, a long-dead family dog, sitting in front of a Christmas tree with a Santa Claus hat perched jauntily on her head; a large studio photograph of Luigi taken in the 1920s in a heavy oval wooden frame—I also can't recall any image of my grandparents as newlyweds. I scan back in time across the various surfaces of the house—the walls, mantels, coffee tables, and chests of drawers—for the phantom picture. Perhaps it was on the little side table next to Gilda's bed—I can almost see a large silver frame between her hairbrush and her jewelry box, but when I try to call up the picture inside, there is only a blank space.

The newly married couple spent their honeymoon in Carolei, the family's native village in Calabria. Luigi was anxious to show off his bride to his parents, Raffaele and Rachele, and Luisa wanted her daughter to meet the family members who never made it across the ocean, mostly those aunts and uncles who were too old to uproot their lives and begin again somewhere else. Like the marriage itself, this was a decision that was made over Gilda's head. She never said where she would have liked to have gone if she had had a choice, or if she had even dared to want something different from what her family had prescribed. Once, when I was in high school, I asked her about her honeymoon. She was alone in the kitchen, making coffee in her beat-up aluminum *macchinato.* We sat down together at the table, and she poured us each a cup.

We like the black coffee, don't we? she said to me as she had many times before. *It's no good, the brown coffee.* Black coffee was what she called espresso, Italian coffee, with milk or without. She was disgusted by the brown, drip-brewed American coffee that her children and grandchildren drank in the mornings. This discernment between the black and the brown, the Italian and the non-Italian, was one of the ways Gilda tried to instill in me a sense of *italianità*—I think it was also a way to prove to herself that I was really "one of us." She heaped spoonfuls of sugar into her cup and then into mine.

She told me that she and Luigi had taken a ship to Napoli, their suitcases heavy with gifts whose luxury was unimaginable in the village: plush blankets and silk stockings and phonograph records of popular American music. Gilda was seasick the entire way there, preferring to stay in their small cabin than to face the endless ocean, the rolling waves. Luigi had met *paesani* on board who were returning to the village for good after decades of work and saved pennies in New York, and he stayed with them on deck, drinking and reminiscing. Gilda remembered a peculiar feeling when they disembarked, her legs trembling against the abrupt solidity of dry land after so many days at sea. Before her the city glittered in the sun, and Vesuvio exhaled gentle wafts of smoke into the bright blue sky. *That was a beautiful country,* she said. *And what about Carolei?* I asked. She frowned and shook her head. *That country I didn't like.* In her memory, Italy was not a single nation, but a series of barely connected countries, with different landscapes, languages, and customs. I could picture her on the train from Napoli to Cosenza, the closest city in Calabria to Carolei. The train would have snaked along the azure coastline, where Gilda must have been awed by the white-sanded beaches and ruined castles. After a few hours, it would have turned into the mountains that soared up from the sea—cooler, darkly forested, and shrouded by fog. This was Luigi's beloved landscape, to which even as an old man he longed to return before he died. Gilda, who had never been out of the city, was terrified. Here she pursed her lips as though she had just remembered the taste of something bitter. She pushed out her chin in that quintessential southern Italian gesture of steel-willed resolve, a gathering of the forces of heart and spirit within oneself in the face of despair. *But I never said nothing.*

They took a mule-drawn carriage from the Byzantine city of Cosenza through meandering mountain roads to Carolei. Gilda would have seen hawks flying over great fir trees, and old women dressed in the traditional way, with long black skirts and black embroidered bodices, and white headdresses draped over their braided hair. She didn't remember much about the village itself, only that it was perched on top of a hill, and the houses were made of pale stone and built closely together, and at night it was terribly cold. Carolei seemed deserted—most of the young men, as well as marriageable daughters and even whole families like the Yacinos had left in search of work, at that time mostly to America and Argentina. She and Luigi stayed with his parents in a tiny house with no electricity or running water. Gilda rose at dawn each morning with her *soggira*—her mother-in-law—and brought water from the well in the center of town. She remembered that the water was always ice-cold and tasted better than any she had ever had. Luigi's mother treated Gilda well enough, and her own relatives fawned over her, telling her how pretty and plump she was. But the hard work and the long quiet nights wore on her. *I cried for the whole three weeks,* she said, chuckling a little. *I couldn't wait to get back to Harlem.*

My father heard these stories as a boy, as did his brother and sister. None of them grew up wanting to go to Italy. Of Calabria, my father always says, *It's just some mules and a dusty old road. What do I want to see that for?* Luigi begged his children to go and visit the ancestral village, especially when he was too old and frail to make the trip himself. He wanted them to keep ties with the family there, but after he and Gilda died, those ties were forgotten. Their children were American Italians—Carolei was as distant and abstract as Mars. East Harlem was their village; 113th Street was their piazza; the family they grew up with, who lived next door or upstairs or down the block, were the only kin that mattered. Their language was New York English mingled with a fading Calabrese, used mostly to communicate to elderly relatives. When Luigi spoke to Gilda in his language, she answered in English, unless they were discussing something they didn't want the children to understand. So even the language of home was divided, between here and "over there," between Luigi's often incomprehensible expectations and Gilda's small rebellions, between past hunger and future aspiration.

Yet if East Harlem was the village transplanted, Luisa was the village embodied. Whatever sense of tradition and connection my father feels to his Italian heritage comes from his grandmother, from the words on her tongue, the labor of her hands, the epic struggle she enacted each day of re-creating life as she had known it in Calabria within the confines of their gray tenement building. Even as that life slipped away from her and from her increasingly American family. *That's what being Italian means to me,* my father says. *All that she was.*

When I first met Luisa, she was living in a tenement apartment on 117th Street, close to the East River. It must have been in the early 1970s, a few years before she died. I can still feel the sense of anticipation, of ceremony, that gathered around that first trip across town. Miriam dressed me in my Sunday clothes, and I remember that my black patent-leather shoes had to be shined. My father and I took a bus across 116th Street, from West Harlem to East Harlem. It seemed to take forever to get there—the bus stopped at every corner. I rode the whole way kneeling on the hard plastic seat, looking out the window. People's faces changed from brown to tan to white, signs on storefronts from English to Spanish to Italian the farther east we went. My father began pointing out landmarks as we passed Third Avenue, the bakery, the firehouse, the barbershop. I noticed even then how different things looked in this other Harlem, the buildings were smaller, fitted tightly together, block after block, like people huddled against each other for warmth. There were many more shops and restaurants, and something I had never noticed before in black Harlem—funeral homes. I already had a basic conception of death, and funeral homes must have existed throughout the neighborhood, but I don't remember ever being aware of them. My father had to explain to me what they were for, and I remember thinking how kind it was for people to build homes for ghosts to keep them from haunting the living. The association stayed with me. We—my father's people, and myself tentatively included—are people who live with the dead in a way that is both intimate and pragmatic.

We got off the bus at First Avenue and stopped at a market to buy Luisa some small offering. *This is called a salumeria,* my father said, taking my hand and leading me inside. *You mean for salami?* I asked. *Very good! What a smart girl!* He smiled, giving me a little pat on the head. He seemed so pleased that I'd made this small connection, and I was proud that I had made him happy. Inside the *salumeria* I was struck by the saturation of color and scent. The blood-red of dried peppers hanging in corners, earthy brown sausages piled on top of the counter, waxy, pendulous cheeses shaped like breasts and teardrops behind the refrigerated glass case. And intimate, pungent smells, as if we were inside a human body, witness to its most secret, private places. I watched the other patrons, broad-hipped women, rough and efficient, shopping for that night's dinner. My father picked up a few items from the shelves, foods that would someday represent comfort to me: a jar of lupini beans, a tin of anchovies, a canister of Medaglia D'Oro coffee.

Holding my father's hand, I closed my eyes and listened to the sound of the voices around me, and I was lulled into a feeling of safety and belonging that my father so often described to me about his own childhood. But as I would learn again and again, safety in my father's world was always provisional. I didn't notice the suspicious, disapproving looks being cast our way, a woman's voice muttering, *vergogna*. My father simply ignored them. Behind the counter, a husky white-aproned man smiled at me and handed me a slice of *sopressatta*. I put it into my mouth and sucked on it, savored it: a concentrated saltiness, dense with *peperoncino* and little chunks of fat. He asked, *Is that your little girl?* and my father gathered in his breath and claimed me, ready or not for the scorn that might follow. My father had brought his illegitimate, biracial child back to the old neighborhood. And I, yellow-skinned, nappy-headed, was too young to understand all that was at stake in this return.

The old neighborhood had changed, my father said, as if noticing for the first time, although he visited his grandmother there a few times a month. He pointed out how the Italian community once stretched from 100th to 120th Streets, from Pleasant to Third Avenues. Now that remembered neighborhood had turned itself inward; a few handfuls of Italian families remained, some shops and restaurants, and the funeral homes, all scattered like stones across five or six blocks. This Harlem was very different from the one I knew, from the old ladies looking out of their windows with their pale, fleshy arms resting on pillows, and the signs above the stores with words I couldn't understand, to the warm, yeasty, and sweet smells coming from the bakery down the street from where Luisa lived. The Latino community had encircled this small knot of Italian life; bodegas, *botanicas*, people speaking Spanish filled in the spaces that had long ago been abandoned for the suburbs by people like my father's family. I couldn't help noticing that I looked a lot like the Puerto Rican kids we passed, playing hopscotch and jacks on the sidewalks, calling out to each other in a blending of Spanish and English.

As we walked to Luisa's apartment my father showed me the traces of his own childhood, the school he went to, the park where he played, the corner where he got caught playing hooky by his father. And the buildings where our relatives lived once upon a time, the old-country people, with names like Mafalda, Domenico, Calogero, Zi Beppina. Staring up at these sooty buildings with their black tangle of fire escapes like knotted hair, I had an overwhelming yet inchoate sense of a past that was somehow mine, but which I had never belonged to and could never retrieve. Yet these fairy-tale names, these tenement buildings, these worn-down streets were my legacy. Passed down from Luisa through the generations, and from my father to me. An inheritance that I would struggle most of my life to claim.

What I remember of Luisa on that day is the vision I'll always have of her: white, white hair, a tiny, stooped body enveloped in widow's black, and those blue eyes. The same eyes as my father, Aunt Angela, and Gilda. Blue, but with a darkness in them, like a cloud passing over the sea. I never got used to my family's eyes, always felt in their blueness not the kindness behind them but the difference between us, and the distance. As I grew up, family members, friends of my father's, sometimes even strangers meeting my father and me for the first time would say about me, *Such a pretty girl, but isn't it a shame she didn't inherit those blue eyes?*

Luisa's apartment was dark and narrow, the rooms hushed and spotless, with heavy wooden furniture and windows closed and covered with layers of crocheted curtains. There were framed photographs everywhere, images that would be misplaced after her death, of distant relatives sent from Italy over the years, and the many American grandchildren. A large photograph of my father—Luisa's favorite—as a baby in a white lace christening gown sat on a long, low dresser in the hallway. Primal smells floated toward us from her kitchen: meat frying, tomatoes simmering. She fed us soon after we arrived: chicken soup with escarole and tiny meatballs, stuffed peppers, homemade regina cookies, rich with sesame and vanilla. I've never forgotten that meal with her, one of the first traditional Italian meals I had ever eaten. I ate everything on my plate—unusual for me, as I always lost my appetite in new situations, among new people—ate even more when she offered seconds and thirds. The flavors were familiar, welcome; there was so much in them that I connected with Miriam's cooking, with her kitchen across town, the saltiness, the heaviness, the feeling of being lulled and caressed by the food as it settled inside you.

After dinner the three of us sat in Luisa's living room, she in an old creaking rocking chair, my father and I on her new couch, covered in plastic like all the couches of my childhood memories, both Italian American and African American. Luisa spoke to my father, and to me, in Calabrese—the words sounded muffled, low, and round, as if her mouth were filled with soft clouds. My father answered her in English, *Yes, Nonna, thank you, Nonna, work is going fine.* At some point Luisa reached out her arms to me and my father gave me a gentle push toward her. I stumbled up to the rocking chair, and she pulled me to her. She smelled of green leaves, basil and parsley and something else, slightly bitter, that I couldn't recognize. She pointed her crooked, knotted finger to her cheek. *Dammi un bacciu.* Give me a kiss. I pressed my lips to her cool, dry skin, inhaled her smell. It's hard to say why I wasn't afraid of her, why I trusted her so easily. Somehow I sensed that she was on my side.

AFTER LUISA'S death in 1976, our family stopped documenting itself in images. It's as if everyone let go of the past in one breath, stopped wanting to preserve it. Maybe it was a surrender to modernity, to the suburbs. But in the loss of the past, the present was set in a kind of suspended animation. Our days and years rushed by without note, significant moments slipped away unmarked. I've always been jealous of friends who have reels of Super-8 film of their family, the grandparents, the mothers and toddlers (the father is always behind the camera), the big family dinners, and the Christmas tree decorating. Or the walls full of photographs down through the generations, all framed and arrayed in a neat narrative: this is who we are, this is where we come from. There are images that I vaguely remember of my family, the few on the walls of the house in New Jersey; a portrait of Luisa, her mother Carmella, Gilda, and Angela together at the christening of Angela's son, Mike; Gilda's boxes of photo albums from the 1950s, of her children's weddings and grandchildren's birthday parties that disappeared after her death. But these are ghost images now, they exist only in my memory. In my mind I see them as the negatives of the developed pictures, the black and white reversed, skin and teeth turned black, the whiteness of the wedding and christening gowns turned funereal, and Luisa's endless widow's dresses glowing white. They are really someone else's memories, and I've only glimpsed them long enough for them all to blur into one another behind my eyes, time collapsing so that the newly born are dying, and Luisa is a young woman again, her feet newly planted on the concrete sidewalks of East Harlem.

My father has a photograph of Luisa that he keeps in tissue paper between the pages of one of his old cookbooks. A French cookbook, from the 1960s, with recipes for blanquette de veau and pommes Anna, foods that have nothing to do with my great-grandmother's life. But most of what my father remembers about his grandmother also involves food, the rituals of cooking and eating, the eternally newfound abundance of the immigrant table. Every now and then, often at my prompting, my father pulls the cookbook off his kitchen shelf, takes out the photograph, and tells me what he can remember. Each time his memories are a little different, some years there are more details, the memories jostled and flung up to the surface. Maybe if I pose my question at the right time in the right words, he'll remember some long-lost moment, some fragment of conversation. Sometimes all he has are the bones of a story about her, and these he gives to me.

When my father was very small, Luisa used to sit him on her knee and sing a version of "This Little Piggie," one that she had known as a child in Calabria. He remembers only the first three lines: *I vogliu pane, nun ci nare, va rubare*—I'm hungry (I want bread), there isn't any, go and steal some. He's lost the end of the rhyme, and so the story circles within him without resolution, fragments of history and comfort and longing orbiting in his mind and always just outside my own grasping reach. This nursery rhyme is different from the rosy-cheeked Anglo version, so full of choices: to eat roast beef or not, to go to market or stay home, to be a good, stoic child and get your reward or to whine and get nothing. The Calabrese version is about having no choices, about a hunger so desperate and a poverty so relentless that there is not even a crumb of bread to satisfy you. It's also about dry-eyed resourcefulness and practical rebellion; the law exploits and excludes you, so it doesn't deserve respect. Steal what you need. Do anything you must to survive.

I hold the photograph in my hands, searching for signs of that great hunger, for other lost endings and forgotten words. It's a family portrait of Luisa, her husband, and their four small children, Gilda and her brothers Joe, Michael, and the baby Frank. There is no date on the photograph, but it must have been taken in the early 1920s. Luisa had arrived in New York from Calabria as an adolescent girl ten years earlier. Carolei was a small village in the Appenine Mountains, close to the vast forests of the Sila Massif, where even today wolves are said to roam. Luisa would tell my father stories about the house she and her family lived in—she, her brothers, and her parents slept in a loft on the top floor; below them was the kitchen, where their few animals—a goat, a pig, and some chickens—slept in the wintertime. She remembered the air inside shimmering with the heat of human and animal bodies and the heavy, oily, sour scent of damp fur and unwashed skin. In the spring and summer months she would pick wild herbs along the hillsides with her mother, who taught her to make medicine from them.

By the time the portrait is taken, she has left that life far behind. She's stout and strong-looking, wearing her best Sunday clothes, a white blouse and long black skirt. A locket hangs from her neck, her wedding ring gleams on her right hand. But there's something odd about the arrangement of the family in this portrait room, the painted backdrop of a large window with tasseled brocade curtains to create the illusion of some kind of grand house, set carelessly against a threadbare Oriental rug that doesn't quite cover the worn floorboards beneath it. Luisa's husband, Salvatore Mancuso, sits with the baby on his lap, while Luisa stands behind him, her hand stiffly placed on his shoulder. She looks out at the camera with cool determination in her downward-tilting eyes; he's almost smirking, as if he got to the chair first and Luisa was left to stand. As if being seated gives him authority in this little kingdom of theirs. The children are lined up in a row in front of them. The older ones wear sailor outfits and lace-up boots, the baby a white gown. Michael, the dark one, is on one end, Gilda, the big sister, holds him tight around the shoulder and also holds her father's hand. Joe stands off a little, away from his father and the baby. All glare suspiciously at the camera. But it's to Luisa's clear eyes that my eyes are drawn, the solidity and centrality of her presence. The hint of contempt on her lips and the distinct falsity of her hand on Salvatore's shoulder. I imagine that she withdraws it without feeling as soon as the flash has gone off and the burst of smoke rises above the photographer.

THE CENSUS record tells me that Luisa's father was the first to emigrate, arriving in East Harlem in 1900. He had found work as a construction laborer and a place to stay in the neighborhood from *paesani* who had come before him. Ten years later he sent for his wife and children. Together they would have crossed the Atlantic on an immigrant ship with hundreds of other people from different regions of Italy, all crowded together in steerage. The same waters that in the previous century had been crossed by millions of Africans, chained to each other in the hulls of slave ships—my maternal ancestors among them. Luisa and her family would have shared a couple of thin cots, and eaten whatever food they could bring with them. I wonder if Luisa ever cried during those long days on the water, or if her eyes remained as cloudless and dry as in her photograph. Maybe she faced the mystery that waited on the other shore, a new life as yet unimaginable, with the same iron will that her descendants would later remember her for. Carmella's health was always poor, and the trip was especially difficult for her. Luisa, the oldest child and only daughter, would have spent much of the time looking after her brothers, taking them up on deck for fresh air while their mother rested below. Not long after the family had settled in America, Carmella went blind.

No one in our family knows anything about Luisa's husband, Salvatore Mancuso. It's not clear if he came from Carolei, or anywhere else in Calabria, or some other part of southern Italy altogether. For some reason, my father feels certain that Luisa married Salvatore in Italy. But the census record says he came to East Harlem in 1903, a few years after Luisa's father. Most likely the two men met there, perhaps on the same job. It's possible that Luisa's father arranged the marriage between Salvatore and his daughter back in Italy—the couple might have been married in Carolei before Luisa and the rest of the family emigrated. The census lists him as a bootblack, a shoeshine man. It was not a profession that brought in a lot of money. When he was not working, he was drinking and gambling. My father remembers stories about how he would spend a whole day's pay at the racetrack and stumble home in the middle of the night, demanding Luisa get up and make him something to eat.

One day my father, Gilda, and I were looking at the photograph of her with her parents and brothers. Her memory had long since succumbed to the ravages of her illness, and I thought that showing her the photograph again might bring back something of what she had lost, some moment of clarity, maybe the recognition of a happier time in her life. She looked at the photograph, her eyes seeming to focus in and out, trying to fix the image in her mind. She pointed to her mother. *Everybody loved her,* Gilda said, smiling. *She was treated alike by everyone, all her neighbors and friends. They still talk about her.* For a moment she was back in East Harlem, in the building bustling with relatives and *paesani.* She looked at her father and it was if a cloud passed across her face. Her eyes darkened and narrowed. *Oh, him—he stinks! He thinks who he is!* My father and I stared at her, startled. *How many beatings did she get from him?* she said, touching the image of her mother's face gently with the tip of her finger. *And I was only a little girl. How many times did I say, you oughta drop dead?*

I never heard this before, my father whispered. We sat together for a long time, the photograph on the kitchen table in front of us. I think my father and I were both waiting for more revelations, but Gilda's face had changed once again—the confused look had returned. *What time is it?* she asked, looking over to the stove. *I should put on the gravy.* My father had only known about his grandfather's drinking, not the violence. At one point, Salvatore abandoned his family, disappearing one day without a word. When he came back—I don't know how long he had been gone—Luisa had changed the locks. She had taken in two boarders to help pay the rent, Genutz' and Capitan. My father still remembers them from when he was a child. *What ginzos those two were,* he says with a chuckle whenever I bring them up. *Really old-country. They did everything for Grandma—they were like her indentured servants.* Luisa forbade anyone in the family to ever speak to Salvatore again. Gilda's brother Frank says of his father, *It was like he was a stranger. If we met on the street, I wouldn't know him.* But my father remembers that Gilda used to take him to see Salvatore when he was a little boy. They'd go to a rooming house a few blocks away where he had been living, and Gilda would bring him food, and tell him what was happening in the family. My father remembers the room his grandfather lived in, a hovel with a single bed and clothes all over the floor. After a while, the two of them had stopped visiting him. My father thinks Salvatore is buried somewhere in Potter's Field.

I look now at the photograph of the Mancuso family and see the seeds of Gilda's defiance, already planted in her fierce stare and the way she holds her father's hand so tightly, grasping his finger with her tiny hand. She would rebel only once more against her mother's wishes. As a young married woman, she had wanted to leave Luigi many times. His drinking frightened her, his carousing humiliated her. After he beat her one night she packed her bags and brought her children to Luisa's apartment. My father remembers his mother and grandmother arguing all night. In the morning, Gilda returned with the children to Luigi. *My grandma was the strong one,* my father says. *She didn't believe my mother could survive on her own.* Gilda never tried to leave again. My father had seen Luigi hit her that night. Nothing would be the same between them. When I was growing up, he and Luigi barely spoke—when they did, it was as if they were on opposite sides of the ocean. Luigi would speak to my father in Calabrese, his words always seeming angry and accusing. My father would answer him in English—in the dull monosyllables that only seem possible in that language.

After her children were grown, Luisa devoted her life to the Madonna of Mount Carmel. She went to the first mass each morning—sometimes she just sat in one of the pews, praying for entire afternoons. In my imagination she kneels before the altar as Gilda did at her wedding. She crosses herself and looks up at the Madonna, smiling. She begins her rosary, fingering the smooth wooden beads one by one until she has made it all the way around. She prays: *O beatissima Vergine Immacolata decoro e splendore del*

*Carmelo, Tu che riguardi con occhio di particolare bontà chi veste il
benedetto Tuo abito, riguarda benignamente anche me e ricoprimi col manto
della Tua materna protezione.* After a while, Luisa begins to speak
openly to the Madonna, telling her of her troubles, her worries,
using the everyday language of her home. It's as if she were a girl
again, telling her own mother what it is that weighs on her heart.
She gazes into the soft brown eyes of the Madonna. Her Italian
eyes. Luisa is sure that the Madonna is looking back, enfolding her
with her own gaze. One morning on her way to mass, Luisa collapsed on the steps of Our Lady of Mount Carmel. She died right
there, just in front of the open doors.

FOR THE PAST three years I've "come back" to East Harlem for the
Feast of the Madonna of Mount Carmel, to walk in the procession
that marks the last night of the celebration. It's twilight. I'm walking in a sea of people, surrounded by the heat of the midsummer
air and the bodies, and the voices singing and chanting. Though I
can't claim to understand their veneration, I'm retracing the steps
of my Italian grandmothers, the circuit they followed years ago,
sometimes barefoot, sometimes on their knees. At the time that
Gilda and Luisa lived in East Harlem, Italian women would carry
huge tiers of lighted candles on their heads as they walked in the
procession, almost as though they were returning home from the
well or the field. Sometimes the candles would be single pieces of
carved wax, shaped like hands or eyes or hearts or breasts, whatever ailing part of the body the woman was praying for. I wonder if
my grandmothers ever carried these candles. It's such an African
image to me, a woman carrying what is most precious on her
head: water, grain, fire.

There are hundreds of people all around me, mostly women,

Italian Americans, and Puerto Ricans, Mexicans and Haitians, all moving together like an exhalation of breath. Skins of every color, the flashing gold of earrings and medallions with the Madonna's image, the flickering of candles that we all hold as we walk slowly down Pleasant Avenue, and turn the corner to 115th Street. We pass the entrance to the church, its stone facade decorated in hundreds of tiny white lights that spell out *Ave Maria*. Farther up the street, Italian American women who still live in this neighborhood unfurl their *biancheria* out the windows.

Everywhere there is singing, songs of devotion to *La Santissima, La Virgen,* voices filling the air in Spanish and Italian, French and Creole. The Haitian women's songs rise above the other voices, they sing in unison, warm and bright, a trembling web of emotion floating up into the air. I don't know the words to any of the songs, in any language, and I walk with a sense of shame that I can't add my voice to those of the women around me. I feel as though I've lost something I never knew I had, something whose presence I can only sense in its absence. We make our way down Second Avenue, our bodies moving and sweating together as the sky grows darker and the candles burn brighter.

We turn back down 116th Street, the main east-west thoroughfare and commercial heart of the area. The traffic has been redirected, we spread out across two lanes. The procession winds past bodegas and funeral homes, the projects and the older apartment buildings, schools and other churches, Catholic, Pentecostal, Baptist. Past the *botanicas,* their windows crowded with sanctified candles and healing herbs, and life-sized images of Catholic saints and African gods; past Mexican taco stands and vegetable vendors selling smoky dried chiles the color of bittersweet chocolate. Past Morrone's Italian Bakery, where the *signora* who came to the neighborhood as a young woman from Campania is still making *friselle,* anisette biscotti, and braided semolina bread topped with sesame seeds. This neighborhood is an almost geological formation, stratified by waves of migration, years of occupation and contestation, different communities who have all called it home. Ahead of us, an opalescent sliver of moon hangs low over the East River.

My candle, a white taper with a paper cone around the bottom to catch the burning wax, sputters as I walk, and I cup my hand around its wavering flame. I've found a place beside the floats that carry the Madonna and the children chosen to be angels this year. The children are many different shades of brown, wearing little white smocks with delicate, shimmering wings attached to their backs that catch and reflect the candlelight around them. They ride ahead of the Madonna, looking back at her and the growing convocation behind her in sleepy awe.

The Madonna glides by on a cloud of white and gold, underneath a canopy topped with a huge, glittering crown. She's surrounded by flowers, no, she's rising up from the flowers themselves as Aphrodite rose from the waves. Her porcelain face gazes down at us, her expression open as a vessel to our dreams and desires. Like the goddess of love she is luminous, opulent. A century ago, women in Italy embroidered with gold thread her brocade gown and cape. She wears gold filigree earrings and a necklace heavy with jewels, and an ornate crown rests on her long, loose brown hair. In one arm she carries the baby Jesus, also crowned and dark-haired, at a small distance from her own body. Not an image of selfless maternity, but one of absolute sovereignty and limitless power. She is the center here, not Christ, not the Father. All around her now the women are praying, crying out: *Maman! Santa Maria!*

We're approaching the church again, walking more and more

slowly now, as if time itself were grinding down and would end when we stopped moving. At the head of the procession, the marching band—young Italian American men playing trumpets and drums and tubas—breaks into the Italian national anthem. The songs of the women grow more intense, punctuated by weeping and whispered prayers and shouts of praise. The Haitian women come up closer, surrounding the Madonna, their arms out-stretched. A canopy of black women's hands above me. *Maman!*

CHAPTER SEVEN

y mother gave me a snapshot my father once sent her from Vietnam—she had found it in one of her old suitcases and hadn't known what to do with it. It's a small black and white shot of him alone, standing in front of a wall made of sandbags. His hair is growing out of a crew cut, and he has a thick mustache. *You look just like him,* my mother said as she handed me the picture, a trace of disappointment barely perceptible in her voice. *No one could ever say he wasn't your father.* On one shoulder he carries two rounds of bullets for a machine gun. His deep-set eyes are closed, almost as if in prayer. He and my mother had exchanged letters throughout the year my father was in the war. She sent him pictures of me, sometimes care packages with his favorite chocolate, a book about Buddhism or jazz. He would tell her about his friends, the meals he managed to cook with his meager supplies, his furloughs in Manila and Seoul. There was an exchange in those letters that I wouldn't know about until thirty years later, something that my parents had deliberately kept a secret from me, a bond of silence and shame between them. Two years after I was born, my father still hadn't told his parents that he had a child.

A FEW MONTHS after Gilda's death, my father gave me his version of the story. The way he tells it, his parents were so distraught when he was dating my mother that he simply never told them when she got pregnant. After I was born, my father decided he needed to wait for the right time to break the news to his parents. He hadn't told them before he left for Vietnam. If he had been killed, they might never have known about me at all. In her letters, my mother demanded that he tell Gilda and Luigi. He wrote back saying that he wanted to do it in person—it was only fair to his parents, after all. He promised he would speak to them as soon as he came home.

Now my father says, *Well, you know I had kind of a hard time when I got home from the war.* Like other returning GI's, he expected a huge welcome, imagined parades and flowers and kisses from pretty girls. Instead people on the street spat at him, called him a murderer. *No way to welcome us home, after we fought for this country* . . . He turned to the comforts he found during the war, disappeared for weeks on end. Heroin was as plentiful in the ghettos of New York as it was in the jungles of Vietnam. Back home, the drug helped him feel like he belonged somewhere; soon his closest friends were other addicts, all lost in some way or another, who found community together in the needle, the spoon, and the lighted match. His addiction was an open secret: everyone in the family knew that there was something terribly wrong with him—his parents, my mother and Miriam, even I could see that shifting and hollow look in his eyes, the extremes of weight loss and gain, the sweaty hands and jimmy leg. For years we explained these things to ourselves,

He's had a hard time or *That's just the way he is.* And when he was late or didn't call or didn't have any money again to contribute for my food or clothes or school, we made more excuses for him.

THERE IS A memory that circles around my mind, like an image projected from a magic lantern, wavering, shadowy, passing just out of sight before I can fully recover it. The image is of a white car pulling up in front of the apartment building in Harlem and a woman, my aunt, stepping out of it. The door opening, her foot touching the pavement. It stops here, and repeats again. I can never sustain the memory long enough for the woman to emerge, long enough to see her face.

Aunt Angela looked the same when she was fifty as she did when she was fifteen: short black hair, striped T-shirts and blue jeans, and lips painted Mustang-convertible red. She had dark blue eyes that flashed black when she was angry. Which was often—she had her father's fierce temper and his exasperating single-mindedness: *a' testa dura,* a hard head, that legendary Calabrese quality. She and Luigi would get into epic battles of will that would rage for days. He wanted her to stay at home and help her mother cook and clean, like a good village girl. But Angela was a new breed, and wasn't going to follow the old ways. She would smoke and stay out and date the toughest boys in the neighborhood as much as she pleased.

Saturday afternoons Aunt Angela would drive down from the Bronx, bringing a toy for me or maybe some clothes her own daughter had grown out of, and grocery money for my mother. I don't know what they talked about, maybe they commiserated about my father, maybe they shared tips about child care or cooking. A single mother like my mother, and like Miriam, Aunt Angela would spend a couple of hours at our apartment, and then she'd have to go back and get dinner ready for her own children. No one else in the family knew about these trips. She must have had to make up stories about shopping and errands to explain her absences. I don't know how to name the relationship between my mother and Aunt Angela, what they were to each other. Was it friendship, kinship?

Miriam, too, is missing from what I know of this story. I vaguely remember that she was usually not home when my father came to visit. She was still furious with him for ruining her daughter, and for not taking responsibility for me. Was she there when Aunt Angela visited? I think she must have been, at least some days. Miriam was protective of my mother, and wary of white people in general. I think she wouldn't allow herself to trust anyone in my father's family for a very long time, even Aunt Angela. Did she serve Aunt Angela coffee, ask after her children? Did she demand that Aunt Angela convince my father to be more responsible to my mother and me? Whatever words and emotions passed between these three women, my birth created some kind of bond between them, and it remained, frayed but not broken, for the rest of their lives. Each one was in a sense alone, juggling jobs and child care and getting by with very little help from the men who had passed through their lives. The situations they found themselves in, so different from what they must have imagined when they were young girls dreaming of their futures, connected them beyond race and culture. They were women who were never meant to cross the borders of their neighborhoods and find each other.

The one constant in this story is my Aunt Angela. Her car pulling up again and again. She was the unbroken thread between me and my father's family. She held my father accountable for his absences and made sure he didn't drift away from me forever. Every time she drove alone from the Bronx and parked her car on that Harlem street she refused the denial that permeated our lives.

And with her visits, the world of my black family and the world of my Italian family began to bleed together around the edges, like watercolor. I can only imagine what she must have looked like to our neighbors, a little white lady with eyes like sapphire. Strutting across the courtyard with that tough girl-gang attitude she had, her thin, determined lips pressed together so they hid the tenderness that flooded just beneath the surface. The black women in hair curlers sitting in their lawn chairs watching their children, just like the women in Aunt Angela's neighborhood, raising their eyebrows as she passed by. And Aunt Angela paying them no mind, walking through the lobby door.

In the early 1970s my father had started dating a woman, Carmen, who lived in the South Bronx. She was Puerto Rican—yet another shame upon the family—but at this point Gilda and Luigi had given up on the idea that he would grow out of his bohemian ways and settle down with a nice Italian girl from the block. The relationship with Carmen was serious; after a few months of dating they moved in together—soon after, they were married. And this is where I came in. My father tells me now that he was beginning to feel more settled in his life. He landed a job as a cook in a fancy restaurant in Manhattan. He had steady money and a place of his own. Soon, he told himself—and my mother, and Miriam— soon he would finally be able to tell his parents about me. *But I wanted to break the news to them gently, to give them time to get used to the idea,* he says. So he told them that I was Carmen's niece. I was three years old.

My father started bringing me to the Bronx to stay overnight. He and Carmen set up a child's bed for me in an alcove of their small apartment. I remember that the walls were painted a dark hippie purple. In the middle of the living room was a giant spool, used to hold electrical cables, that my father found at a construction site. He painted it black and used it as a table. There were plants everywhere, sprouting avocado seeds in water glasses, hanging ferns, clusters of aloe like beseeching hands along the windowsills. There were two Persian cats, one white, one gray—my father has always had cats for pets, sometimes as many as four at a time in the cramped spaces he's always lived in. He feels an affinity with cats that he could never find with people, a kind of stillness in them, a lack of judgment or expectation. He used to brush those two Persians for what seemed like hours, and kiss their foreheads, and whisper a kind of baby talk to them.

I don't know when I first met Gilda and Luigi, what the circumstances were when I was introduced as Carmen's niece. I suppose they saw my fawn-colored skin that so closely matched Carmen's, and just looked past the obvious family resemblance. My father describes the whole thing as a joke, almost, a comedy of errors. A case of mistaken identity that we can all laugh about now. Only I can't find the humor in it. My father has long since forgotten when he told them the truth about me, but he says that first he went to Luisa. She asked him solemnly, *Is this child really of your blood?* He didn't deny it. *Then she is sangu du sangu meu,* she pronounced. Blood of my blood. If she accepted it, he says, everyone else had to go along with it, too. My father does remember Gilda's reaction, how she looked at him as if in shock, and then burst into tears. He told me once that what had really hurt her was the fact that he had lied to her. That he had kept such a big secret from the family. It seemed to me that he had left something out of the story. *Was it because I was black?* I asked him one day. My father was quiet for a moment. *You have to understand,* he began. *My mother was from a different world. She couldn't get her head around having a black grandchild, so she just saw you as Italian. Because I was light,* I added. He looked at me a little impatiently. *Yeah, I guess so. But what if I wasn't so light?* I insisted. *It's over now, and in the end they loved you. That's all that matters, isn't it?*

I have an image of my father's parents coming through a door, and me hiding behind my father. He tries to pull me out from behind him and get me to greet them, and I bury my face in my hands, shake my head no. I'm afraid of the sound of Luigi's voice. How loud he is, and Gilda, too, and how different their voices are from any others I have ever heard. Are they speaking another language? Round sounds float up around them when they talk, it's a little like music. And they're round, too, both of them short and wide, Luigi with his beer belly, Gilda and her huge, pillowy bosom. I remember, too, the color black, Gilda's immense black leather purse, Luigi's slicked-back black hair and black shoes. From this time forward, black would always be an Italian color for me, the black of tradition, of old age and mourning, the black of the soil, and the black of purgatory. My own purgatory.

When was it that Gilda and Luigi ceased to be my father's parents and instead became my grandparents? I have a couple of fuzzy memories from that time. My father bringing me to visit them. Gilda pinching my cheek, exclaiming, *Oh, she's getting so big.* The feeling of her fingers against my cheek, warm and moist. Luigi calling me over to sit on his lap. He bounces me on his knee and calls me "Papano," the same thing he calls my cousin Marie. And a huge black bird flapping its wings, looking at me through shiny button eyes. Luigi had a Mynah bird—it lived on a perch in the living room. There was no cage—I remember there were newspapers on the floor around the base of the perch to catch its droppings. Luigi would take my hand and bring me over to the bird—I don't remember what he had named it—and he would make it talk to me in his language. *Somanabeetch,* the bird would squawk, *Va fangool!*, the equivalent of go fuck yourself. I would erupt into giggles, and Luigi would give the bird a treat.

I HAVE A handful of photographs from when I was a child, that Carmen had set aside for me after she and my father split up. She told me that she knew someday I'd come and ask her for them, ask her for some documentary proof that my childhood existed at all. The first is my favorite—it must have been taken when I was around six. It's one of those old, black and white photo booth pictures; usually there are four to a strip, but this is the only one Carmen had. I'm alone in the booth, probably kneeling on the little stool to be high enough for the camera to get my face and not just the top of my head. I'm grinning impishly up into the lens, and my dark eyes are shining. My hair is done in two Afro puffs, standing out from either side of my head like giant earmuffs. I don't remember taking this picture, or who was waiting for me outside the booth, though most likely it was Carmen and my father. The emulsion on the photograph has worn almost completely away— only my head is still visible, and part of the striped background. Underneath is the white, now yellowing contact paper, giving the image of my face the look of an island floating in a blank sea. The edges of the lingering emulsion are jagged and curled upward, and it crumbles into a fine black dust if my finger brushes against them. It is as if the child that I was is disappearing before my eyes. My image of myself literally coming apart. It's not possible anymore to know the whole story behind the picture—what I was wearing, where I was, who else was there with me—yet there is a center that holds against all those scattered facts. A truth among many competing, disappearing truths: my face, looking straight into the eye of the camera. My own gaze open, unwavering.

I would have been in the first grade at the time this picture was taken. The previous year, I had gone to kindergarten at Riverside Cathedral School. It was a private school, attached to a politically progressive Protestant church that served the community up at Columbia University. The building was designed in the Gothic style, with a high bell tower at one end. I think the school was actually in the basement, although for years afterward I imagined that it was up in that tower, at the very top. It was something out of one of my fairy stories, like the tower where Rapunzel let down her rope of blond hair. I wonder now what I would have made of such a story, the little girl with the Afro puffs, whose hair did not flow down like a river but sprang up and out in all directions, each corkscrew with its own life, its own will? Or did I imagine the bell tower was a fortress where I was not imprisoned, as Rapunzel had been, but protected?

I can still picture the classroom, a rectangular space with a long wooden table in the center, at which we children sat. I can smell the scent of Pla-Doh and finger paint, and see our drawings taped along the pastel-colored walls. The class was integrated; most of my classmates were the children of Columbia professors and graduate students. My mother tells me that there were children from all over the world there, which is why she chose the school for me. *Our family was multicultural before there was even a word for it,* she told me when I asked her about the school. *I wanted you to be exposed to other children who were different, like you.* I remember my teacher was from India. She wore brilliantly colored silk saris that she let me touch sometimes—the fabric was so thin, so delicate, that it seemed to be woven from clouds. She wore a single black braid that reached almost to her knees—Rapunzel's dark sister. I loved this woman, my first teacher. She was the one who taught me the alphabet, and praised my first attempts at writing my name, getting the Y to go forward instead of backward after much practice. I remember very clearly clinging to her when it was time to go home for the day. I would cry desperately as my mother or Miriam or Aunt Gladys pried my small arms from her waist.

The one friend I can still recall from my class was a little white boy with an African name, Masamba. His hair was the color of wheat, and his eyes were such a pale, watery blue I wondered if he could really see out of them. His mother was a hippie who had once spent some time in Africa in the Peace Corps. She and my mother became friends, and I spent many nights sleeping at their house, watched by a nanny while the two of them went out on double dates. It was with Masamba that I played the inevitable game of doctor, pulling down our pants in his mother's closet and peering at each other's "pee-pees," though never daring to touch.

I don't know how my mother was able to afford the Cathedral school. It must have been a significant drain on her resources, because in the first grade I found myself in a public elementary school two blocks from Miriam's apartment. No one gave me a reason for the abrupt change, and I never saw my teacher or Masamba again. PS 231 was a large brick building with metal grates covering all the windows. Inside there was a labyrinth of white tile-covered hallways and classrooms with rows of students each at his or her own desk. My first few months there are a blur—I remember at first the other kids in my class called me whitey: *Hey, whitey, why don't you go back to white-people land?* I kept to myself but developed a secret crush on Kevin, a popular boy with black cherry skin and a perfect halo of an Afro. He already walked like a little man, leaning forward with one step and dipping back with the next, his hands stuffed in his front pockets. He had the tenderest eyes I had ever seen. I quietly mooned over him for a year, but I never got up the nerve to talk to him.

My first and only friend was a quiet girl named Tanisha whose desk was in front of mine. She wore cornrows and pretty flowered dresses that her mother made for her, and she had glasses with thick lenses that she hated but I thought made her look smart. For months I begged Miriam to get me a pair of glasses so I could look like just like her. We had two teachers, both black women. One was there full-time, she was soft-spoken and patient even when the class became unruly. A young student teacher came a few days a week to help her, or to cover when she was out sick. When the student teacher had the class alone, the students would disobey her, throw spitballs, and drop their books on the floor. Once she ran out of the room in tears and everybody laughed—even me, though I felt sorry for her. The principal burst into the room a few minutes later, and made us put our heads on our desks until it was time to go home.

Across the top of the wall in front of the classroom there were plaques with all the letters of the alphabet printed in perfect, looping cursive. We had to practice our own handwriting in light blue composition books, careful not to let our pencils go above the middle dotted line for lowercase letters, and the unbroken lines for capital letters. Our textbook was *Fun with Dick and Jane*. We would practice reading out loud the same sentences again and again, following the story of heroic Dick and his blond little sister Jane, who lived in the suburbs in a big house, where their mother wore an apron and their father smoked a pipe. I remember when we first started reading the book I got very confused: I began to think that all boys were supposed to have brown hair and white skin, and all girls blond hair and white skin, and all cats were female and all dogs male. I couldn't reconcile the world of *Fun with Dick and Jane* with our Harlem classroom and our black, brown, and yellow skin. I must have felt that the book was in some way authoritative—it was handed to us by our own teachers so that learning itself seemed inseparable from learning that world. At such a young age I couldn't see that there was something wrong with the book, that it excluded most children in the "real" world. It was we who were somehow wrong, because we didn't look like Dick and Jane or live in a house like theirs.

One day after school I was in my room practicing a new word I had learned from some of the other kids: "motherfucker." Miriam passed by and heard me. Miriam never cursed, neither did my mother—to this day, "heck" is the strongest swear word I've ever heard come out of her mouth. On my father's side, it was only Luigi who cursed, and usually not in English. I had no idea what the "fucker" part of the word meant—I just liked the hard sound as it shot out of my mouth. Miriam came into my room, stood at the door for a moment, staring at me as if she suddenly didn't recognize me. She grabbed my hand and dragged me into the bathroom. *Where did you learn that filth?* she demanded as she pulled me toward the sink and turned on the water. Holding me by the collar, she began to wash my mouth out with soap. I shrieked as she rubbed the chalky bar of Ivory around my tongue and across my teeth, gagged as the bubbles rose up out of my mouth and ran down my chin. *Only bad children use that kind of language,* she said to me, her voice cracking with rage. When it was over, she held me close to her, so tight that I could feel her trembling. I cried bitterly against her bosom. *I'm sorry,* she whispered. *I'm so sorry, baby.* My mouth stayed clean for a long, long time.

THE FOLLOWING September I started the second grade at the Convent of the Sacred Heart. I had just begun to like to the idea of returning to PS 231. My best friend was there, and by the time summer break began, the other kids had stopped calling me whitey.

And it was nice that the school was so close to our apartment—often Aunt Gladys would pick me up at lunchtime and take me home for a sandwich or a big bowl of chicken noodle soup, with thick egg noodles and lots of parsley, the way only she could make it. More than anything, I was an accommodating child—after the initial shock, I got used to any situation. Sacred Heart, though, was like nothing I'd ever known before. The school was housed in two connected nineteenth-century mansions on Fifth Avenue—the previous owner had bequeathed them to the convent at his death. The buildings were immense, made of great white stone blocks. Each building had four floors, connected by vast marble staircases and cage elevators. A ballroom with walls of mirrored glass served as the lunchroom and ballet studio. The library was paneled in mahogany, and the chapel was filled with light from the floor-to-ceiling windows that opened out onto the street. The students, all girls, were the children of wealthy Catholics, among them Kennedys, European royalty, sugar barons from the Philippines.

Somehow, my mother and Miriam combined forces to get me into the school on a scholarship, and they found a way to pay for whatever wasn't covered. My mother doesn't remember how they first heard of Sacred Heart, only that Miriam was adamant that I go to private school as my mother had done, that I had the same benefits as she had. Gilda and my father were pushing for Catholic school. The first day of second grade Miriam woke me up at six A.M. I thudded out of bed and into the bath in a fog. I hated waking up early to begin with—it was bad enough that schools everywhere began at eight in the morning, but at least PS 231 was just a short walk away. This particular morning, and each day for the next two years, I would be bused to school. Miriam made me a bowl of oatmeal with extra brown sugar, and told me how wonderful my new school would be. After breakfast we hurried downstairs, Miriam with her cup of coffee in hand, and waited outside the building for the small yellow bus to arrive. On the ride from Harlem to the school, I smoothed down my new uniform, a gray jumper with a pleated skirt, covered with a red gingham pinafore. I watched as familiar sights flew past the window: the dark edges of the park, the two new apartment towers shaped like tubes of lipstick that Miriam hated for their ugliness. I was the only one almost the whole way there—this didn't make me feel special, that I had the whole bus to myself. It felt shameful to be surrounded by all those empty seats, to stare at the back of the bus driver's head and not know what to say.

The bus let me off at the entrance of the school, a domed enclosure where horse-drawn carriages and their coachmen once waited for their princely employers to descend. A stream of other girls and their mothers were already filing in. As each of us entered, we had to curtsy to the headmistress and shake her hand. *Good morning, Sister Desseaux*—the deep bend of the knee, the childish singsong of the greeting are forever ingrained in my body's memory. Sister Dessaux looked like a saintly Jackie O, with hair black and gleaming as a raven's wing. As did some of the other nuns, she wore secular clothes, modest skirts and twinset sweaters. I remember a strand of pearls around her neck, although that doesn't seem possible, as nuns are supposed to take a vow of poverty. Some of the other nuns still wore the ancient habit of their order, which had originated in France more than two hundred years before and had spread, by the end of the nineteenth century, throughout the colonized world. Years later I would be astounded that my Indian mother-in-law had also gone to Sacred Heart, this one in Lahore. These traditional nuns terrified me—they flitted through the halls, in rustling black robes and veils, with stiff white wimples that framed their scowling faces like ghostly flowers. You had to curtsy to them, too, and keep your eyes averted out of respect, though I was happy not to have to look into their silent, faraway eyes.

That first day someone—I think it was Sister Desseaux, though I'm not sure anymore—brought me into my new classroom. I remember being introduced to the class and being pushed toward the only other black girl in the room. *Look, Beverley, another little black girl for you to play with,* the sister exclaimed. I looked at them both in a panic. Did that mean I wasn't supposed to play with my other classmates? For the first couple of weeks I attached myself to Beverley, afraid to even speak to the other girls in case I got in trouble. Beverley was also bused in from Harlem. That first day her grandmother had brought her to school, but from then on we would ride together each morning. Beverley had been at Sacred Heart since kindergarten—she had already made friends with most of the other girls, though I don't know how easy or difficult it had been for her. She was one of the tallest girls in the class, and she had a laugh like Woody Woodpecker—she would throw her head back and out would come this incredible joyous rat-a-tat-tat. I wonder now if it was her way of overcoming the isolation of being different, to play the class clown, to disarm everyone around her with laughter before they could reject her out of hand.

I eventually formed a few other tentative friendships, none as close as the one I would develop with Beverley. There was one girl, Susan, who had long bone-straight blond hair and cornflower blue eyes. I asked her one day during playtime if I could comb her hair with the red plastic comb she always carried with her. It was the first time I had ever touched a white person's hair. It was smooth and fine, though I'm not sure if I liked the feeling of it. It felt foreign and unreal between my fingers, like the hair of a doll. I decided she needed some curls, and I twirled her hair around the comb. When I tried to unroll it, I found that her hair and the comb were tangled together. I tugged and tugged, but the blond strands just pulled tighter against the teeth of the comb. We both started crying and yelling for the teacher to come help us. I remember the hot tears running down my cheeks, and a cold, jangling fear that I would be punished for hurting such a perfect little girl. Eventually, they had to cut Susan's hair where it was tangled. It was many years before I dared to touch another white girl's hair.

Our teacher was a young woman who had once been a nun. She was twenty-three, a magical number that stuck with me. I liked the idea of becoming twenty-three one day—I thought when I hit that number, I would officially become a grown-up. We would bombard her with questions about why she had left the convent: *Don't you miss Jesus and Mary and all the angels? Is God mad at you now?* She explained to us that there were different ways to believe, and she left to explore what they were. She described heaven as a place where you would live forever your happiest memory, and I imagined heaven as a vast file cabinet, where everyone had their own drawer, and inside the darkness of the drawer they would remember their own happiest moment. I couldn't picture it as a place that was filled with light, with people floating on clouds playing harps. Heaven had to be dark in my mind, a place of infinite secrets. I had been thinking a lot about heaven after I heard Miriam and Aunt Gladys talking about a little boy who lived down the block from us, who was killed when the rusty fire escape he had been playing on had collapsed and fallen six floors to the street. *It's a dirty shame,* Aunt Gladys sighed. *A child's life ain't worth a dime anymore.*

The next day at recess I stood in front of the huge wooden crucifix that hung against a tapestry on the first floor of the lower school. A carved and painted wooden Jesus hung from the cross, real iron nails piercing his palms and feet. His body was alarmingly pale and thin, the ribs jutting from his sides, the cloth that covered his private parts draped low on his bony hips. His head hung limply to one side. I looked up at his sad, tired eyes and asked him to make sure the little boy who fell off the building made it safely to heaven. Bowing my head, I mumbled three Our Fathers and three Hail Marys just to make sure Jesus took my prayer seriously. A few feet away from the crucifix there was a niche that held a relic of the saint who had founded the convent—a tooth and a fragment of bone—suspended within an ornate gilt frame. The profoundly ordinary remains of a human body long disintegrated, now become holy. I see myself as a seven-year-old girl in that mysterious setting, my hands clasped tightly together, praying for the soul of a little boy I didn't know to a God who I wasn't sure was listening. The world I knew was full of broken bodies: a child crushed against the pavement surrounded by shards of rusted iron, girls forced to become women too soon, their bodies cracked open by men who didn't care what they were taking away. And I was discovering that God Himself was just a broken man.

THE SECOND OF the photographs Carmen gave me shows me standing with my mother and father in front of the steps of a church. It's the only photograph I have ever seen of my parents together. I remember when it was taken: I was on my way to be baptized into the Catholic faith. Preparations had been under way at school for my class to celebrate our first Holy Communion. We were all so excited—the nuns buzzed around us, telling us what an important moment this was in our lives, serious and joyful all at once. There would be a special mass for us in the chapel, and we would get to wear our own white dresses with veils, just as if we were getting married. We had begun practicing for the ceremony, walking single file down the center aisle of the chapel, pretending to receive the host—*the body of Christ, amen*—and making our way down the side aisles back to our pews. Somehow word got out that I had not been baptized—I'm not sure how this happened, but I remember that one day, after I had been babbling to my mother about how I couldn't wait to try on my new Communion dress, she turned to me and said I wouldn't be having Communion with the other girls. *Maybe next year,* she said with a shrug.

I began to sob, probably imagining I had done something wrong and my punishment was that I had to stay home when everyone else got to celebrate. Was it because I had played snow globe the week before with Miriam's talcum powder, shaking it over my head as I twirled around the room, pretending to be a famous ice skater? Miriam had caught me just as I was emptying out the last of the powder onto my face, sticking my tongue out as if I were catching snowflakes. Miriam had called Aunt Gladys in and the two of them stared incomprehensibly at me. I was completely covered in treacly-smelling white, as were the floor and my bed. *That child has gone and lost her mind,* Miriam said, and they both began to laugh until tears ran from their eyes.

My mother explained that I couldn't have Communion without being baptized. I yelled at her, demanding to know why she and my father didn't do what my classmates' parents had done for them. It was the first time I had rebelled against my parents, the first time I questioned out loud, and with anger, the haphazardness of my upbringing. I'm sure now that this outburst wasn't the result of religious devotion, although later I would go through a period of wanting to be a nun when I grew up, as most Catholic girls do at some point or another. And I did pray every night, kneeling in front of my bed, *if I should die before I wake . . .*

It was my grandmothers who had given me a sense of the mystery, the magic behind religious faith. Miriam insisted that everyone in her house say grace before dinner. We would sit at the kitchen table, or in the living room, with our TV trays in front of us, and bow our heads as she began, *Thank you O Lord for this food which we are about to receive in Christ Jesus' name amen.* Even though I mumbled through the prayer, the words all flowing indecipherably together, *inchristjesusnameamen,* I grew up feeling that each meal with Miriam was a gift. The food she made each night—the pot roasts braised in wine and the luxurious macaroni and cheese, the fried chicken whose salty, earthy smell perfumed the house for days afterward—came from her labor and her love, and from all the sacrifices that went into putting the food on the table. Once I took it into my body, it became part of me—I lived because of the sacrifices of others, mostly in ways I would never see.

Most Sundays, Miriam would take me uptown to the Abyssinian Baptist Church. She would put on one of her best dresses and a new hat, or an old one with a new band of feathers or velvet, a different flower pinned against it. She always made sure I had special Sunday dresses to wear, one for each season, with thick, itchy matching tights, and white patent-leather shoes. We would sit high up in the balcony—*This is the best view,* Miriam would say, settling into her seat and looking around for people she knew. There were always people coming over to say hello, women with hats that were even more fabulous than Miriam's, hats in colors that matched their dresses, hats trimmed in gold brocade, hats with swaths of fine tulle like bright confections on their heads. And men in suits, with deep, smooth voices, who called her Sister Miriam. The whole church would buzz with warm brown voices: the exchange of greetings and compliments, embraces and condolences.

The preacher would begin his sermon, pacing back and forth in front of the congregation. I don't remember what he spoke about—most of the sermon probably went over my head—but I can still hear his voice rising with the energy around us, and the triumphant singing of the choir washing over us like fire. Stout middle-aged women and frail old ladies would leap spontaneously out of their chairs, weeping and laughing, shouting, *Hallelujah!* Sometimes ribbons of mysterious words would stream out of their mouths, and then they'd fall down in a faint, other women rushing over to help them. Miriam never seemed to get the spirit in that way, but once in a while, she too would shout *Hallelujah* and *Amen* and *Yes, Lord, yes Sweet Jesus.* Then she would sit back into her chair, beaming and fanning herself with a paper fan that had the face of Jesus on one side. This Jesus had clean, shiny blond hair and smiled serenely, his blue eyes sparkling like a movie star's—so unlike that Catholic Jesus of my new school and my Italian family, who suffered and wept and bled.

We never said grace before meals at Gilda's. Yet there was a deeply ceremonial, reverential aura around the food we ate at her table. Gilda and Luigi had known hunger in a way that Miriam hadn't. Nothing was wasted—Gilda used to keep the heels of bread in an old coffee tin, and when she had collected enough, she would grind them to make bread crumbs. In Italy, when her own mother was lucky enough to eat pasta, she would sprinkle bread crumbs over it for flavor, because her family couldn't afford cheese. There was something both holy and voluptuous in this pragmatism, in the resourcefulness that Luisa passed on to Gilda, who carried it with her from the Old World of Italian Harlem to the Promised Land of the suburbs.

Gilda kept an altar on her bedroom dresser in the Bronx, figures of the Madonna and Saint Anthony on a handmade lace cloth. I remember a votive candle burning there, which she lit each morning when she woke up. Sometimes when we visited her, and she and Luigi and my father were caught up in their own conversation, I would slip into her room. I'd stare at the candle's serpentine flame, put my face close to it to breathe in its heat. Once I tried to play with the figures, to make the Madonna and Saint Anthony dance with each other as though they were dolls. Gilda came in to call me to lunch, and when she saw what I was doing, she grabbed them out of my hands. *You can't touch this place,* she said, pushing me away from the altar. *This is where God stays.* It was a lesson I never forgot. The mystical and the intimate were not separate things. You did not have to look for God in a church, and you did not need a priest to guide you to the sacred.

Priests were not well loved in my father's family—Luigi believed that in Italy the Church supported the interests of the wealthy landowners and offered nothing to the poor, and even in New York he refused to step foot in a church unless it was for a marriage, a baptism, or a funeral. God, the saints, the Madonna lived in Gilda's bedroom, the most profane of spaces. And she could call them forth whenever she wanted, as long as she kept the flame burning.

I grew up with a vision of her faith as primordial, sorcerous. It would take many years before I began to understand that faith in the context of Luisa's intense devotion to the Madonna and her role as a healer, and the ladies at Miriam's church who spoke in tongues, and the clairvoyance of my Aunt Virginia, for whom the veil between the living and the dead was so terribly thin. Ultimately, it was female power itself that was sacred. It didn't really matter if you prayed to God or to his Mother, if your Jesus was bloody or clean. Once I videotaped Gilda peeling chestnuts that she had just roasted. I focused only on her deeply wrinkled hands, and the deft way she used a sharp knife to pry the first bit of hard, fragrant shell away from the nut inside. With just a few quick motions she pulled the rest of the shell apart and released the steaming meat of the chestnut onto her old wooden chopping board. Simple gestures that she had performed hundreds of times in her long life, as had her mother, and her grandmother, and all the women in her family down through the generations. Watching the tape later I could see that the mystery, the magic, and the faith were all in those hands— in the gestures, the bodies, the hungers of women.

As a seven-year-old girl, all I wanted was to be like everybody else. I wanted to walk in a line with the other girls in my class, wear the same white dress, share the same experience. I was tired of standing out, always being the different one, the special case. My fuss about being excluded from first Communion must have had an effect. My father said later that Gilda had also demanded they baptize me, arguing with both him and my mother until they relented. She had been horrified from the beginning that I had not been baptized when I was born—it was unthinkable, completely outside her range of experience that any child in her family could remain so long outside the state of grace. Yet she would have been equally horrified if my father had legally married my mother—it would have been just as impossible for her to imagine her family including a black woman.

She even called Miriam, probably one of the first conversations they had ever had. Gilda must have felt sure that Miriam would be sympathetic, that as a grandmother she would only want the best for me. It must have been a strange discussion, the two women on either end of the telephone line—their voices so unfamiliar to each other—measuring their words, trying to remain polite. It was also probably the first time Gilda so forcefully and publicly staked a claim on me, asserted her position as grandmother after so long playing the role of bystander. I wonder now if Miriam felt at all threatened, or if she welcomed Gilda's intervention, thinking it was about time that she, too, took some responsibility for me.

My mother told me that most of the churches she and my father approached refused to baptize me because my parents were not married when I was born, and in the eyes of God bastards did not have the same rights as legitimate children. But at the last minute they found a church that would perform the ritual as an emergency measure before the Communion ceremony. So along with the rest of my class that year, I did get to make my first Holy Communion. I wore the white dress with the delicate tulle veil that hung down my back, and perhaps I did feel like a child bride of Christ. In the chapel we sang a French song, kind of an anthem for the Sacred Heart order: *Oui je le croix, oui je le croix / elle est immaculée, elle est immaculée.* Yes, I believe it. She is immaculate. During mass I stood and knelt at the right times, remembered all the words to our prayers. I watched as our priest poured red wine into a golden goblet in front of the marble altar, which was covered with lace. *Take this wine and drink of it, for this is my blood.*

When the time came, I stood before the priest, a kind, soft-eyed man who beamed at me as if I were his own child. I stuck my tongue out and he put the host in my mouth. *Amen,* I whispered, and crossed myself. After the ceremony many of the nuns, and our teacher, and Sister Desseaux, crowded around us, telling us how perfectly we had performed. Sister Desseaux hugged me and told me she was proud of me. Waiting among the parents and siblings of my classmates were Miriam and my mother and father. They gave me a bouquet of flowers and kept talking about how beautiful it had all been. Nothing more was said between us about the struggles of the weeks before. Gilda did not come down to Manhattan for the Communion, but that weekend in the Bronx she made lasagne in my honor. After dinner she gave me a set of red crystal rosary beads. *Read your card,* she said, pushing it into my hands. *For a very special little girl, love Grandma.*

The photograph I have was taken the week before. I had just been baptized inside the dark stone church. I don't remember the actual ceremony—the whole thing must have taken around fifteen minutes. I vaguely recall standing on some kind of footstool in front of the baptismal font, the priest dripping holy water on my forehead and making the sign of the cross over me. Carmen was with us that day; I had taken her middle name, Maria, as my own baptism name. She was the one who took the photograph—I don't know if any were taken with her and me together. My parents are standing next to each other—already a miracle at this point—smiling uncomfortably for the camera. My father has an Afro and a long beard, and his face seems plumper than usual. He's wearing a Norwegian fisherman's sweater under a forest green blazer with lapels that reach to his shoulders like angel's wings. I don't think I've ever seen him in a blazer since. My mother's hair is straightened into a kind of pre–Farrah Fawcett flip. Her eyebrows are plucked thin, as was the fashion then—they look almost as if they were drawn onto her face with a fine-point pen. She has on a dark dress that I can't quite make out, and over that a short fur jacket with soaring shoulder pads that looks like it might have been a thrift-store find from the 1940s.

I'm standing in front of them in a buff-colored winter jacket; a white wool cap completely covers my hair. My father's huge hand is on my flat chest, and I'm grasping it at the wrist with one hand. My other hand is clasped between my mother's hands, held close to her belly. I have an impatient look on my face, as if I just wanted to get it over with. I must have known that such a moment, with my parents together and holding me close to them, couldn't last very long. Maybe I realized that after the picture was taken, we would most likely all go our separate ways: one of them would take me back uptown to Miriam's, my father and Carmen would head back to the Bronx, and my mother would hail a cab downtown.

By this time my mother had a new boyfriend, and it was serious. His name was Paolo and he came from Italy—he was some kind of businessman she met when she was doing fashion shows in Milan. I had already met him many times—the two of them would take me to the movies, and to Serendipity, a fancy restaurant famous for its frozen hot chocolates, served to pampered children in huge frosty goblets. Paolo wore expensive suits and always paid with a flourish, pulling hundred-dollar bills from his wallet like they were play money. Right away I saw that he was Italian in a different way than my father and my grandfather. His lilting accent was nothing like the gruff roundness of Luigi's Calabrese. He had straight, light brown hair and a long, narrow nose, and a straight line where his lips were supposed to be. *He's a better kind of Italian,* my mother had once said to me after an outing with Paolo. I don't think she understood that in my eyes, better than my father meant better than me as well.

A few months later, my mother and Miriam sat me down in the living room in Harlem. Miriam stood at the window with her arms crossed against her bosom. *Your mother has decided to move to Europe,* she said coldly, glancing at my mother, who sat next to me and held my hand. Before I could think of what to say, they began arguing bitterly. Miriam accused my mother of abandoning me, of being irresponsible and acting like a foolish teenager. My mother said that all Miriam cared about was the money my mother brought in, that she wanted my mother to be alone for the rest of her life and die an old maid. *Just like you,* my mother said, her voice low and flat.

My mother must have realized that she had been unnecessarily cruel. Miriam sat down in a chair across from us and shook her head, her hands limp in her lap. My mother went over and kissed her on the forehead, something I had never seen her do before. She said to both of us, *This is the best way I know to give us all a better life.* I don't remember how I felt, if it even registered in my mind how far away Europe was. Even as an adult, I don't think the emotional impact of my mother's decision has fully hit me. I see my little-girl self just shrugging and going off to play in my room. It was 1973, and my mother was still only in her mid-twenties. She had been modeling steadily for a number of years, and had been to Europe many times, posing in magazines and even getting bit parts in Italian films. Some of her girlfriends—other black models who were making their way in the industry—also had children who lived with their grandmothers, in Georgia, Chicago, New Orleans, Brooklyn. Many of them lived in Paris or Milan, and flew home every couple of months to visit. They would send money home to their mothers, more money than anyone in their families had ever seen. Their children went to private schools, and had savings accounts set aside for them for college. I'd see some of these kids once in a while, when my mother took me to their birthday parties. They were mostly younger than me, and they always seemed to be only children without brothers or sisters. The parties would consist of a couple of these children and a roomful of glamorous women and deep-voiced men smoking cigarettes. I remember the feeling of tugging on my mother's dress, of looking up at her as she talked to her friends. They all seemed so impossibly tall, so far away. I remember, too, the dazed look of the birthday girl or boy, seated in front of a huge birthday cake, seemingly overwhelmed by the pile of gifts wrapped in vibrantly colored paper that invariably stood in a corner, waiting to be opened. *Make a wish,* the mother would say, and the child would blow out the candles as the adults clapped and raised their glasses of wine or champagne.

My mother moved to Rome later that year. She would live there through much of the 1970s and '80s. On holidays she would come back to visit, staying in the spare bedroom in Harlem until she convinced Paolo to rent a small apartment downtown so they could spend more time in New York. She would bring me beautiful velvet dresses and gold jewelry, and envelopes of money that she would slip quietly into Miriam's hands. Each time she came back felt, at least to me, like a celebration—she was like a fairy princess, returning to her kingdom after a long exile. She wore tight jeans and high-heeled shoes, diamond rings on her fingers, and at one point a white fur coat, just like the one she saw so long ago in the window at Saks. I remember sitting on her lap one time, playing with the ropes of gold necklaces she wore. On one of them hung two small pendants, gold figurines with outstretched arms that locked together so they would become a single piece. One of the figurines had a penis, although I'm sure I didn't realize at the time what it was. The other had a hole for a mouth, and also holes between its legs and on its backside. Mesmerized, I kept sticking the one figurine into the other in as many combinations as I could come up with. I remember my mother laughing nervously. *I got this in Greece, on a beautiful island,* she said, prying my hands from the necklace. One Christmas my mother gave me a white rabbit-fur jacket to match hers. She gave Miriam a gold watch whose face was an ancient Roman coin. Miriam was wearing it the day she died, twenty years later.

I don't know how Miriam felt about these visits, though she did tell me long after that she was relieved that my mother could afford to keep me at Sacred Heart. *You're the only thing that mattered to me,* she said. All I ever heard the two of them talk about at that time, besides me, was where my mother had traveled to and where she was going next. Miriam seemed excited to hear about the glamorous islands and glittering cities of Europe, especially Paris. *One day we'll go to Paris, just you and me,* she'd say to me. I dreamed that one day I'd be rich like my mother so I could take Miriam there. And then one Christmas, when I was thirteen, my mother surprised Miriam and me with a trip to northern Italy. It was a blur of tour-bus visits to the centers of ancient, bewildering cities and their landmarks: the Colosseum, the Milan Cathedral, Michelangelo's David. It was my first visit to Italy, so different from the Italian American world I knew back home. But it was my mother's gift to me, a new connection to the country of my paternal ancestors. And with this gift, my increased desire, or need, to claim my *italianità*. It would be almost twenty years before I would see the southern landscape that my great-grandmother Luisa and my grandfather Luigi had left behind, the place where part of me began.

THE THIRD photograph shows me and Carmen's nephew, Little Caesar, at her and my father's apartment in the Bronx. They were living above the bar where Luigi worked, a squat, narrow two-story building with two apartments on the second floor. Aunt Angela lived with her kids in one of the apartments after her divorce— when the other one became vacant, my father and Carmen moved in. I had my own room there, painted a pale yellow, that looked directly onto the covered tracks of the elevated 6 train. Every few minutes, the train would roar by, shaking the whole building.

The photograph was taken at Christmas in 1973. Little Caesar and I are sitting in our pajamas in front of a huge tree laden with tinsel and surrounded by brightly wrapped presents. In the background you can see the windows covered with bamboo shades, and an orange candle on a small pedestal sitting on a Chinese cabinet made of dark, carved wood. I'm wearing a prim nightgown of light blue flannel. My hair is in two braids, fuzzy from sleep and tied at the tops with pink yarn ribbons. I have an expression on my face that I clearly got from my father—he has a photograph of himself as a child in the 1950s with the same look—chin tucked in, eyes peering upward, uncertain smile. Little Caesar, two years younger than me, has his head cocked to one side, his black eyes shining mischievously. It was the Christmas after my Communion. I was spending more time in the Bronx, weekends and most of the summer. On holidays, I would stay over the night before and celebrate with my father's family during the following day. In the early evening, my father would drive me back to Miriam's, where we would have our own celebration.

Each Christmas I would open two sets of presents in front of two trees. My father's would be a real fir decorated with thin glass bulbs etched with gold sparkles that Luisa had given him from her own collection. Miriam had a small white plastic tree, shaped like a fir, hung with blue and silver bulbs. Each Christmas Eve she would set it up on top of the TV console in the living room. There would be two Christmas feasts. After spending the morning at my father's house, we'd walk to over Gilda's, where we'd have baked ziti and braciole, and the special cookies that Gilda learned to make from Luisa, balls of vanilla-scented dough fried in olive oil and soaked in honey. For dinner at Miriam's, there would be ham glazed with rum and brown sugar or a goose with oyster stuffing, buttermilk biscuits drenched in butter, yams baked with a marshmallow crust, and an angel food cake with chocolate frosting for dessert. I would fall asleep soon after, my stomach churning and reeling with the mix of flavors from the two meals—the sugar and the salt, the olive oil and the butter, all the different forms of sharp and spicy, savory and sweet.

Behind me in the photograph is a large lumpy item covered by an Indian print bedspread, with a card and a bow pinned precariously on the front. I don't know if I had dared to believe that morning that it was the drum kit I had been begging my father for. I remember tearing the cloth away and seeing the pearly drums and the shining cymbal, and being completely speechless. After a few minutes of staring at the drums, I ran to my father and threw my arms around him—he and Carmen had tears in their eyes. I jumped on the stool and began banging the bass drum with the foot pedal and crashing the cymbal with the sticks that were taped to the cloth, which now lay in a heap on the floor. *That's enough for now, honey, it's still a little too early,* my father said as he covered his ears. I had dreamed of those drums since the summer, when my father had started play jazz records for me, telling me about the different musicians as they did their solos. He'd play Miles and Coltrane, Monk and Mingus, Pharoah Sanders and Rashaan Roland Kirk. *Now listen to Max Roach on the drums,* he'd instruct me, or Elvin Jones, or his favorite, Rashied Ali. My father had a vibraphone against one wall of the apartment, and often he'd play along with the record, hitting the metal keys with soft mallets and humming along with the notes. Carmen would play her own records: Eddie Palmieri, Tito Puente, the Last Poets. Their apartment was always full of music, no matter what time it was or what they were doing. Whatever kind of music it was, the drums seemed to stand out for me. My ear would always follow the snare or the conga or the tabla. My cousin Mike would blast rock music from his room in Aunt Angela's apartment, Led Zeppelin, Black Sabbath, the Who. Sometimes I'd wander over to his door and listen. Mike would be stretched out on the shag rug, reading a motorcycle magazine. He'd notice me there, smile sweetly, and say, *Hey, kid.* I knew enough not to step over the threshold, so I'd just hover there, lost in the music. Mike had taped a poster of Keith Moon above his bed, grinning demonically, his hands just about to crash down on his drums. I was hooked.

It seems incongruous now that the timid, sweet girl I was in that photograph could tear so ferociously at my little drum kit, an instrument that I had only ever known men and boys to play. Yet tear and pound at them I did, every chance I had. After Christmas, my father had set the drums up in my room. Whenever a 6 train would rumble by, I would try to keep time to its rhythm, and see if I could make more noise than it did. I shared the room with Little Caesar whenever he was visiting, and each time I played, he would run out shrieking. Little Caesar's parents were in Puerto Rico a lot of the time—usually he stayed with Carmen's mother and went to school near her apartment in the South Bronx. Carmen thought it was a good idea for the two of us only children to spend time together, so, like me, he'd stay over on weekends. It was nice having him around—I started to see him as my own little brother, fighting with him over toys, getting into wrestling matches, letting him ride on my back, pretending he was a cowboy and I was his horse. Carmen would make us Puerto Rican food a lot of the time, *chuletas* and *platanos,* rice and beans. Little Caesar didn't know a lot of English—mostly we communicated in a kind of baby talk—and at the table he and Carmen would speak Spanish, which my father understood. He would translate what they were saying to me, and after a while I'd try to follow what they were saying on my own, picking up words here and there that I had already learned, recognizing others that sounded like Italian words I'd heard from Luigi. We were a makeshift, temporary family on those weekends, suspended between three languages and many desires around the idea of "home." Not exactly *Fun with Dick and Jane,* but a family nonetheless.

Eventually Little Caesar's father took him back to Puerto Rico. I remember missing him for a long time afterward. I was eight years old, in the third grade. Something was beginning to shift in me that year. I was happy at Sacred Heart—I had more friends and was doing well in my lessons. During the weekdays I would wear my uniform, practice my French and piano and ballet at school, then come home to Harlem and jump double Dutch with the other girls. But I would take the ribbons and barrettes out of my hair as soon as I was out of Miriam's sight, and all I wanted to wear when I wasn't in school were my Toughskins dungarees. After Little Caesar left I started tagging along with my cousin Marie whenever I was in the Bronx. Marie had short feathered hair and had just had her ears pierced, something I was not allowed to do until I was her age. She wore faded blue jeans with a comb sticking out of the back pocket, and Converse sneakers. I started to dress like her, and when I was alone in my room I even practiced chewing gum like her and talking her tough white-girl talk.

I'm sure Aunt Angela made her look out for me—I think she even earned a few dollars as my unofficial babysitter each time she took me out with her and her friends. It was only when we were older that I saw how kind and good-hearted Marie was behind her streetwise facade, just like her mother. And like me, she was the only daughter of a father who wasn't around a lot; we were both trying to figure out how to love and be loved in an environment where that was not always easy. One of the first times she took me out with her, we went to an industrial area a few blocks from our building, where the neighborhood kids played handball against the brick walls of the factory buildings. It was a fall weekend, and the sun was already fading by the afternoon. The other kids were all white, mostly Italian American and Irish American. I remember being so excited just to be with Marie, to be a big girl like her who didn't need a grown-up to watch over me.

Marie joined the game, but I stayed off to the side, too shy to ask if I could play. One of the boys looked over at me and shouted, *Hey, I think there's a nigger here!* The other kids turned around and

stared at me. My heart pounded against my chest, as if it were trying to escape from my body. I was ready to run away as fast as I
could, but Marie came and stood next to me. *She's not a nigger,* she
told them. *She's my cousin, Kym. It's just dark outside.* The kids went
back to their game, and they never called me that word again, at
least not to my face. Marie claimed me, protected me, though she
could only do that by denying who and what I was. But she had
found a way to save me from being beaten up, and save face among
her friends at the same time. And I had passed for white, barely—
this time. What would happen to me when it wasn't dark outside?
It was a tightrope Marie and I would walk together many times in
the years to come.

Marie's best friend, Lina, lived two blocks away in an apartment building that was even more ramshackle than ours. Her family was large and exuberantly loud. Lina had four brothers, Joey,
Sal, and two older boys I never met. She also had a little sister my
age, named Theresa. Their father worked all the time, a day job and
a night job, and we rarely saw him. Their mother had tender, wea-
ried eyes, and she spoke with an accent much like Luigi's. Whenever Marie and I came to visit, she would be mending the kids'
clothes, or soothing their upset stomachs, or cleaning their endless
cuts and scrapes. They didn't seem to have much money—the siblings wore each other's hand-me-downs, and their furniture was
threadbare, worn in after years of jumping contests and wrestling
matches. Lina's mother would always invite us to stay for lunch or
dinner, even though it looked like they never had much food. The
whole family was dark-skinned, "Siggie"-dark, people in the neighborhood would say, meaning Sicilian. Sal, the youngest, was the
darkest of all. He was just a year younger than me, and Marie and
Lina would always try to push us together. *You guys are gonna get
married someday,* one of them would tease, and they'd start singing,

Kymmie and Sallie siiting in a tree, k-i-s-s-i-n-g! Sal and I would stay as far apart from each other as we could manage so we wouldn't be taunted—we barely even looked at each other sometimes. We wouldn't have been able to name our shame in the girls' teasing— was it the embarrassment of having a sexuality forced on us that we weren't prepared for, or was it about our dark skin, how we were singled out and forced together because of it?

In spite of the teasing, I felt comfortable at their house—at home, in a way. Their mother never treated me like an outsider. Sometimes she'd pinch my cheeks and say, *What a pretty girl you are.* I think I started to see myself as part of the same raucous unit as Lina and her siblings—Marie and I spent most of our free time with them, sleeping over on Saturday nights, squeezed into Lina and Theresa's twin beds with them, dancing with the brothers to Elton John records. I don't remember them ever hanging out with other kids in the neighborhood—it's as if they had lived in their own world. Maybe it was because they seemed to live just outside the watchful gaze of the community, a little outside its rules, that they were able to make a place in their world for me.

I grew close to Theresa during my eighth and ninth summers. We were the same age, both our birthdays in February. Theresa had large, dark eyes and dimples in her cheeks. She talked with a kind of lisp that made her seem younger than she really was. We'd go everywhere together, holding hands—everyone called us the Bobbsey twins, but we didn't care. We spent a lot of time at an old cement factory down near where the other kids played handball. There was a pile of dirt, maybe two stories high, that was used to make the cement before the factory closed down. The two of us would go there with her brothers early in the morning and play King of the Mountain, scrambling up the dirt hill trying be the first to get to the top. A big part of the game was to prevent anyone else from getting close to the mountaintop, and we'd push and kick each other down the hill as we climbed, shrieking like banshees. I don't think I had ever felt less aware of my blackness and my femaleness than on those days. Rolling in the dirt, getting knocked in the eye by someone's elbow, skinning my knees, landing on the ground as another body came down on top of me—I was very much in my body, banged up and bruised, but at the same time I felt an exhilarating freedom from it. It was as if I could forget my difference—the way it insisted itself and was insisted upon—and just be a body among other bodies. Jumping double Dutch in Harlem I had reveled in being a black girl among other black girls—was it that my difference didn't exist, that I was exactly what I was supposed to be, or was there more room for gradations of difference within the wide embrace of blackness itself? At the same time, in Harlem I was painfully conscious of my female body's vulnerability to danger. Miriam still wouldn't allow me to cross the street by myself, let alone leave the building unsupervised. In the Bronx, boys and girls my age and younger roamed the neighborhood, playing stickball and Ring-O-Leevio together in the street long after the sun went down.

Was this the safety that my father talked about feeling in East Harlem? If it was, it did not come without a price. There were always stories about gang fights between kids from different parts of the neighborhood. Once a boy was stabbed to death a few blocks away by a rival gang member, and Aunt Angela kept Marie and me in the house for a week. Gang kids would rob local stores, breaking in during the night and taking whatever money they could find, smashing the windows behind them. Years later my father would look back on that time and tell me, *You know, they say the blacks didn't care about their neighborhoods, but we were the same way—no one ever wants to talk about that.* A lot of things weren't talked about. I first learned the word *omertà* from Luigi. One time a relative had been found with a bullet in his head. For weeks whenever we visited Gilda's, I would hear the adults whispering about it. I would pick up fragments of their conversations, *What a shame* and *Santamariagesu*. Luigi would just sit at the table, staring into his glass of wine and sighing deeply. No one ever talked openly about these things, certainly no one ever explained them to me. Silence was both a burden and an honor. And the worst thing anyone could be was a rat, a person who broke the silence.

Between our building and Lina and Theresa's there was an old German Lutheran church surrounded by a vast cemetery. An iron gate separated the cemetery from the street, but you could easily see through to the graves overrun with wild grass, and the marble mausoleums guarded by statues of weeping angels. The church had been there for more than a century, and some of the headstones were crumbling or leaning backward, the names of the dead long worn away by the wind and the rain, and later by the pollution from the ceaseless traffic along Westchester Avenue. Theresa and I would run past it on the way to or from each other's houses, holding our breath and trying not to look at the graves or the hulking darkness of the church. To us, the church was already jinxed because it wasn't Catholic, which in that Italian neighborhood made it almost satanic. When it got dark we were afraid that ghosts would come out of the ground and snatch us through the gate if we didn't move fast enough. The last image I have of Theresa is of her running to her house, shaking her long brown hair as if she were saying no to the ghosts, no to the graves. And the moonlight bouncing off her hair. She was giggling as she ran, and I called after her, *Go, go, go—you're almost home!* A few years later, when we no longer lived nearby, Aunt Angela told me that she heard Theresa had been raped one night, on her way home.

CHAPTER EIGHT

One day in the beginning of August 1975, my father drove me down to Harlem. When we got to Miriam's and rang the bell, my mother opened the door. I was surprised to see her, and I threw my arms around her. She wasn't usually in New York in the summer—for a moment I thought maybe she had moved back, that we'd all be together again. Instead of dropping me off at the door, my father came inside. The two of them led me to the living room, where Miriam was waiting. She looked sad and tired, as if she hadn't slept the night before. I realized that something must be terribly wrong, and I stood by her and held her hand. My mother and father sat next to each other on the couch. My mother began, *How would you like to move with your father to a nice big house and have the same last name as him?*

My father had never given me his surname—I don't know whether he didn't want to, or whether my mother didn't want me to have it. My mother once told me that she named me Kym Ly after a beautiful Korean friend she had at the time she had been dating my father, named Kim Lee. She had added the *y*'s in a flash of inspiration—*much more interesting that way, don't you think?* How my surname was decided remains a secret between my parents, another instance of *It was too long ago, I can't remember anymore.* For nine years my last name had been the same as my mother's and Miriam's. I had often been embarrassed when people asked me why I didn't have the same last name as my father, and I never knew what to say. *It will be easier this way,* my father offered. *Sure, okay,* I said, accepting the pragmatism of the situation.

I asked about the big house. Were we moving somewhere else in the Bronx, maybe to a two-family attached house made of yellow brick like the one my father's uncles and their wives lived in? It turned out that the new house was in New Jersey, a place I had never seen and could not imagine. Miriam spoke after being silent for most of the conversation. *You'll be in the country, with lots of fresh air—just wait, you'll love it.* The month before, Aunt Gladys and I had been robbed at gunpoint on the stairs on our way up to the apartment. The man grabbed Aunt Gladys's purse and shook the contents onto the dirty tile floor. He took her wallet, with its few dollars and her Social Security card, and ran down the stairs, laughing. I had never seen a gun before in real life, and I remember thinking how heavy it looked. We made our way back up to the apartment—Aunt Gladys was shaking and crying, and I tried to comfort her, to convince her that we were safe, though I didn't believe it myself. A few days later, she packed her bags and left for Pittsburgh.

I didn't connect our being robbed in Harlem, or the growing gang violence in the Bronx, with the idea of moving. Instead I panicked at the thought of leaving Miriam. Weekends and summers in the Bronx were one thing, but the possibility of never seeing her again was unbearable. *Just think about it,* she said to me, patting my cheek and smiling her wide, worn-out smile.

One morning at Miriam's toward the end of August, I discovered my suitcase and some boxes in the foyer. I ran into the kitchen, where Miriam was making my favorite breakfast, waffles and bacon with extra butter and syrup. I asked her where we were going, imagining the two of us on some adventure. She told me that my father was on his way to pick me up, that today was the day I was moving with him to the big house. I cried inconsolably throughout breakfast. Miriam just held me and told me it would be okay, that I could come and visit her whenever I wanted. *I'm not going anywhere,* she said. My father came to get me, and Miriam helped us bring my things downstairs. He loaded them into his car, and we drove in near silence back to the Bronx.

We left for New Jersey that afternoon in a caravan, my father, Carmen, Aunt Angela, Marie, Gilda, Luigi, and me packed into two cars, with a moving van following behind us. Mike stayed behind—at seventeen he decided to move in with his girlfriend instead of having to leave her. Most of the other Ragusas and Mancusos—Gilda and Luigi's brothers and their wives, their children and grandchildren—would remain in the Bronx, many of them until they died.

I remember going through the Lincoln Tunnel for the first time, frightened by the thought that we were actually underneath the Hudson River. I remember noticing the dividing line in the middle of the tunnel—on one side in bold white letters it said New York, on the other, New Jersey—I couldn't figure out how they could divide the river in half. We emerged from the tunnel that day part of the middle class, on our way to living the American Dream. A house in the suburbs, two cars, a garage, and a backyard. I, too, emerged as something new: Kym Ragusa. Not exactly a black girl, not exactly an Italian girl. I didn't know the term "white flight" until I was an adult, but here I was, incongruously enough, part of the white ethnic exodus from the city. My father and Carmen were quiet most of the way there. In the car ahead of us, I could see Gilda and Luigi, Aunt Angela and Marie talking excitedly and gesturing out the windows. I don't think any of us knew what we were in for.

The landscape of New Jersey was like nothing I had ever seen: wild swamps and factories spewing stinking gases into the sky gave way to endless miles of highway, which eventually took us to our new town, Maplewood, with its neatly paved streets and blocks of houses with freshly cut lawns and American flags waving from poles near the doors. I was used to seeing American flags at school—even at Sacred Heart we had to recite the Pledge of Allegiance after the Our Father each morning. I wondered if people in Maplewood came out of their houses in their pajamas and saluted the flag before breakfast. I couldn't wait to see our own house, imagined it was one of the white shingled ones with the shiny black shutters on the windows, and rosebushes along the front walk; when we finally pulled up to the house on Boyden Avenue, my heart sank.

It was large and boxy, the bottom half painted a dirty-snow white and the top a dark gunmetal gray, giving it a gloomy, dejected appearance. An enclosed porch with a sloping roof was patched onto the front of the house; a thorny tangle of bushes—not rosebushes—crowded against the bottom of the porch, taking up what little there was of the front lawn. A chimney rose from the pointed gray roof—I envisioned our family sitting before the fireplace on cold winter nights, roasting marshmallows—until I found out that the chimney had been blocked up long ago. To the side of the house was a driveway that led to the garage, also painted that awful gray. But when we pulled into the driveway and I saw the small backyard, I was sold. I jumped out of the car and rolled in the grass, inhaling its crisp green smell. Luigi came out and joined me, walking the perimeter of the yard and calling out all the things he planned to grow: *Pomodori! Zucchini! Melanzane!*

It took hours to unload all of our boxes and furniture and bring them into the house. I was the only one who hadn't been there before—the rest of the family had driven up to see it a couple of months before. I wandered through the rooms filled with stacks of boxes, taped-together suitcases, upended furniture covered with sheets. It seemed impossible to me that we would ever be able to unpack it all, that this wilderness could be transformed into a real home. I remember suddenly feeling timid, wondering if I really belonged there after all. For the rest of the evening I hid in the empty fireplace, until Carmen called me to dinner. When I came into the kitchen, I saw that the big wooden table that had been in Gilda's house in the Bronx had been set up in a nook by the back door. Everyone was already sitting down, tearing into plates of cold cuts and loaves of Italian bread. *Come sit down, honey,* Gilda called to me, *I made you a sandwich.* The windows behind the table faced out onto the backyard. I looked out into the darkness, startled by the sound of crickets that I hadn't noticed before. Inside it was warm and bright—everyone was laughing about the trip that day, how long it had taken, how bad the smell had been when we came out of the tunnel. *The armpit of America, that's us,* my father said.

A curious memory I have about moving day. I'm sure I remember that a group of neighborhood kids pelted the windows of our front porch with tomatoes and eggs, yelling and jeering as we watched from inside. I can see the blood-red of the tomatoes and the vomit yellow of the eggs as they hit the windows. My father says no such thing happened, that I must have made it up. Yet I remember it so clearly—and afterward I was afraid to go to school in case I ran into any of those kids. For the longest time I thought my father had just forgotten, or that he was denying it to protect me somehow from a bad memory. But when I asked Carmen and Marie, they didn't remember either. Maybe it really was a dream, the first dream I had in the new house. So many of my emotions around that time are lost to me—what I hoped for in our new life, what I feared. But this memory, or dream, or image, has stayed with me all these years, as clear as if it had happened yesterday. It tells me something of my anxiety about belonging. Did it really happen? I guess I'll never know the truth. But when I think about it, I can almost hear those kids yelling the word "nigger" through all the splatter.

THE LAST photograph Carmen gave me is a school portrait of my fourth-grade class. The Clinton School was a public, coed elementary school a few blocks from our house. The composition of the class describes the neighborhood as a whole: mostly Italian American and Irish American, and a handful of Jewish kids, whose families had made it into the suburbs a generation or two before mine. Twenty-four students stand in three orderly rows, smiling for the camera. Our teacher, a chubby woman with long brown hair, stands to one side. I don't remember her at all, and I'm shocked by how young she looks, more like a babysitter than a teacher. The kids are all wearing generic 1970s clothing, bought from places like Sears and Marshalls: ProKeds, knit vests, lots of plaid and orange.

Maplewood was not a wealthy community, at least on our side of town. The houses were relatively modest, with small yards like afterthoughts, crowded with jungle gyms and bicycles left lying in the grass. Irvington Avenue, the border with Newark Heights, was two blocks from our house. On the other side were rows of housing projects blocked off from the street by a chain-link fence. You would stand on our side of Irvington and be surrounded by white people, mowing their lawns, barbecuing, having bake sales on the sidewalks, and you'd look across the street and see only black people, women coming from the grocery store, young men playing basketball, girls jumping double Dutch.

On the other side of Maplewood was where the rich people lived. I barely ever saw that part of town, except at Christmas, when Aunt Angela would drive Gilda, Marie, and me there to see the elaborate decorations of the houses. We would cruise the streets in Aunt Angela's white 1950s Oldsmobile, marveling at the pristine mansions with life-sized Santas waving from sleighs on the roofs, and sweeping lawns lined with reindeer made of hundreds of tiny lights. The kids who lived in these houses didn't go to Clinton, or to Marie's public junior high school in nearby South Orange, where some of the students had recently been killed by a speeding train while they were hanging out drinking on the tracks.

There was one other black student in my class—I think there were three or four of us in the whole school. He's standing in the last row in the picture, between two blond boys. He has deep brown skin and a small Afro, and he's wearing a sky-blue suit, unlike most of the other boys, who wear T-shirts or turtlenecks. I can imagine his mother picking out the suit for him the night before the photograph was taken—knowing that he would be seen differently than his white classmates, that he would be expected to be sloppy, unruly, to not fit in. She made sure that he looked better than any of those white kids. So that the picture is more a portrait of her love, protection, and defiance than a simple documentation of our fourth-grade class. The boy's name was Robert, and we weren't friends. Like most of the kids in the picture, I barely have any memory of him. I think now that I went out of my way to avoid him, to not call attention to my own blackness by associating myself with him. And I wonder how conscious this decision was in my nine-year-old mind, how deliberate my averted eyes when we passed each other in the schoolyard.

I'm in the center of the front row; the plaque that announces the name of the school, the date, our class, and our teacher is directly in front of me—it looks like it's leaning against my knees. I have on a bright white sweater and blue jeans—by then I refused to wear anything else. My skin is clearly darker than everyone else's except Robert's, although I'm almost the same color as Judy, a Jewish girl I was friends with who's sitting a few spaces away—a kind of faded caramel color against the pink of the other faces. Next to me is Jeannie, my best friend. She lived up the street with her parents and little sister; her parents were Polish and spoke with thick accents. Her mother was always trying to sell their house, but it seemed no one wanted to buy it. For the next twenty years, long after I had lost touch with Jeannie, there would be a for sale sign stuck in the middle of their front lawn.

I wonder now where Jeannie's mother wanted to go—after all, what could have been better than where they already were, in their corner-lot house with its shag rugs and crystal figurines in cabinets of polished glass? I wonder, too, what it was like for Jeannie to come home to that for sale sign every day, the constant threat of upheaval announcing itself in shrill red letters, as if to remind her never to get too comfortable. Jeannie fought with her parents constantly, barely tolerated her sister. Her expression in the photograph is how she always looked, how I'll always remember her: she's the only one who isn't smiling. Her round, milky face is covered with freckles, and her brown, wavy hair hangs down over her shoulders. When I look at her now I can just barely make out her mother's face behind her own: the small, dark, agitated eyes, the pink downward-turning mouth.

In the photograph my hair is long and straight, hanging past my shoulders. I've pushed part of it back behind one ear, so that the ear juts out disconcertingly. It's as though I thought I wouldn't be able to hear through my hair, that I was afraid I'd miss some important instruction. My mother took me to get my hair straightened for the first time right around the time she told me I was going to live with my father. The adults had all agreed that Carmen would have an easier time with my hair if it were "relaxed," that I could even begin to care for it myself. At the time, I didn't know about their consultation—my mother only recently told me the story. I remember going with her in a taxi to what my mother called the hair salon; she explained what was going to happen and how I would look afterward. *Just wait till you see yourself,* she exclaimed as we got out of the car. I was terribly excited that I was going to be pretty like her—my mother's hair was always straightened or braided into extensions that hung down to her waist. I'm sure I must have also imagined I'd look more like my friend Theresa and the girls in my class at Sacred Heart, that it would help me blend in. In Harlem, it was usually the older girls who had their hair straightened. I must have thought it would give me a new cachet in the building, that I would seem somehow older and tougher.

My mother had a friend, Antoinette, who had her own salon. She had come to New York from Mississippi and had made a name for herself doing hair for black actresses, singers, and models. Chez Antoinette was on the second floor of a nondescript office building in midtown; I couldn't imagine how a hair salon could be in such a place—the beauty parlors I knew, in Harlem and the Bronx, were always storefronts, where ladies sat uncomfortably under hair dryers by the windows and you could watch them as they read their magazines and squirmed under the heat.

When the elevator opened onto the second floor, it was as if we had stepped onto a tropical island. The salon spanned the entire space; there were plants everywhere, and potted trees, and the walls were papered with bamboo leaves and brilliantly colored parrots. There were black women everywhere, walking around in loose, silky robes tied casually at their waists. Their skin was every possible shade of brown, and they all had thinly plucked eyebrows like my mother, and lips painted blackberry, or claret, or shimmery gold. Tall, elegant black men stood behind some of the chairs, cutting other women's hair—I stared at them, awed by the speed and grace of their hands as they snipped, by the fluid, dreamlike way they talked and laughed. I didn't know how to name their difference: if I had met a gay man before that day, I wouldn't have known it, and didn't really have a conception of sexuality other than the assumption that girls liked boys, and boys liked girls. I had heard the word "faggot" thrown around in both Harlem and the Bronx—I didn't know what it meant but I knew it was something pretty bad. I had seen how boys would call each other that word, black boys and Italian boys, seen how they'd fight over it, rolling on the ground trying to pin each other down, punching each other in the face until they bled. In Antoinette's salon, though, there was no sense of violence, of fear. The men there embraced each other, moved with a confidence and strength that I hadn't seen in any of the men of my childhood.

My mother greeted almost everyone there, kissing the men and women on both cheeks. *Ciao, honey,* they'd call out to each other, *don't you look fine.* Antoinette was a thin, petite woman with long straight hair cascading around her face; she didn't wear any makeup on her smooth, nut-brown skin, but her dress was a flowing blue silk, and like my mother she wore diamond rings and many thin gold necklaces of different lengths. She spoke with a soft Southern accent, and right away she called me *my baby.* In the years that I would go to her to get my hair "done," she would always hug me and kiss me as if I were her own daughter—*Isn't my baby getting big!* I would cringe through each of these greetings, embarrassed at being seen as a baby, though the alternative, when Antoinette began referring to me as a "young lady," was perhaps even more distressing. When I started to enter puberty, a couple of years after this first visit, I began to notice my mother and Antoinette commiserating about what it was like to raise a daughter—Antoinette's own daughter was just a couple of years younger than me.

I'm sitting in the chair in front of the mirror, with my mother and Antoinette standing behind me, both looking at me, my mother shaking her head forlornly. *It's too soon,* she says to Antoinette as if I can't hear her. *It can't be happening now.* I'm twelve years old, and my forehead is covered with red pimples and a greasy shine. I look at my reflection. The mirror is surrounded by small bright lights, like backstage in a theater. I don't know what "it" is, don't know that "it" is about to hit me like a freight train. *You just got to accept it, girl,* Antoinette tells my mother, as she gently strokes my hair. *It happened to you, it's happening to your daughter. That's the way it is.* I try to catch my mother's eye through the mirror, but she isn't looking at me anymore. There is a melancholy, faraway expression on her face.

That first day, the day that my virgin hair would be straightened for the first time, Antoinette sat me in one of the chairs, raising it up with a little foot pump at its base. She wrapped a towel around my neck and laid another one across my shoulders. To start, she combed out my hair, tugging on the knots with one of those long-handled combs that are kept in jars of antiseptic blue liquid. I flinched and cried out whenever she hit a snarl. *Keep still, now,* she said in her honeyed voice, *this won't take too long.* After my hair was combed it stood out in every direction like the mane of some wild and frightened animal. Antoinette smoothed it down with warm oil, which she then rubbed into my scalp. The oil dripped down over my forehead and into my ears, and I kept trying to catch the drops with my towel, with Antoinette admonishing me to be still each time. Next she put on a pair of latex gloves and slathered the lye-based straightener, thick and creamy like mayonniase, onto my head. The smell was chemical, not made pretty and feminine with perfume, but harsh and abrasive like something used to clean hospital floors. She combed it through my hair in sections, with special attention to the roots, where she put on extra. The roots were the most defiant part, pushing up out of my scalp in tiny, fierce coils. The euphemisms for the straightening—to relax the hair, to loosen the curl—were aimed at just this resistance.

Soon my scalp began to burn, at first a slow tingling, then suddenly the sensation that my head was on fire. Alarmed, I begged her to rinse it out. *Just a minute more, I'm almost done,* Antoinette said impatiently. *Wait till you see how pretty you look.* The same thing my mother had told me. After a few more painful minutes, Antoinette led me to a room in the back, where she washed my hair, scrubbing the scalp so vigorously I thought my hair would fall out. When she was done, she rubbed my hair dry with a clean towel. I reached under the towel to touch it—I hadn't yet seen the metamorphosis. It was slippery, like wet string. We went back to the mirror, and Antoinette combed my hair once more, the comb sliding easily through it. Abracadabra! My hair was bone straight, the roots laying flat and limp against my scalp, the ends reaching toward my shoulder blades. After sitting me under the hair dryer with huge rollers pinned tightly against my scalp and then brushing my hair in long, dramatic strokes, Antoinette released me to my mother. On the way back up to Harlem, I shook my head and my hair swirled around my face. In a way, I liked it. My new hair did make me feel older—no more ribbons and pigtails—but it was disconcerting how vulnerable and exposed my scalp now seemed, and I was distracted by the feeling of my hair brushing against my shoulders, like there were spiders crawling over me.

Once a week in Maplewood, Carmen would wash my hair and roll it up in big curlers, sitting me between her legs. I'd have to sleep in the rollers, my head resting painfully on the hard plastic, the roots of my hair yanked away from my scalp, hairpins poking into my ears. This reality was a sobering challenge to my growing persona as a tomboy, with its attendant fantasy, in my case, of racelessness.

FROM THE FIRST day of school, I spent most of the time with Jeannie. I remember the teacher introducing me to the class that morning. There was a banner in gold letters above the teacher's desk that said, *Welcome Kim Lee!* One girl raised her hand and said to the teacher, *I thought she was a Chinese girl.* There were no Asian Americans at the school, and apparently the class was hoping I'd be their first. After that case of mistaken identity, though, life went relatively smoothly there. I wasn't one of the popular kids, but I got along well enough with them—they seemed to treat me with a kind of detached respect, though I'm not sure why. I don't remember anyone calling me a nigger, though it must have happened at one point or another, and maybe I've just found a way to forget it. Most likely my classmates didn't know what to make of me at all, with my dark-but-not-too-dark skin and my long straightened hair, my "Chinese" first name and my Italian last name. What I do remember is being called *hey Ragusa* by the boys in my class—it was uncool for them to call each other or the girls by their first names. I answered to *hey Ragusa* with an odd familiarity and slightly embarrassed pride. I had only had my father's surname for a few months, but I clung to it as if it were irrefutable proof of my belonging, both at school and at home.

I was small and uncoordinated, and was always one of the last to be picked for games like kickball, which I hated anyway. Even at nine years old, I was disgusted by the mindless cruelties of gym class, the way the popular kids would hound those who were weaker, laughing at the skinny ones, the ones with the thick eyeglasses, the black ones, the Jewish ones, who waited on the sidelines to be chosen. Jeannie was also one of the last to be picked—we'd pretend we didn't care, scowling against the wall and acting bored, secretly hoping that at least we'd end up on the same team.

Shauna was Jeannie's best friend before she met me. She came from a large Irish American family—I think she had six brothers and sisters. They lived in a yellow Tudor-style house across the street from me. I hadn't spoken much to her at school; she had her own group of friends and sat way at the back of the classroom. There must have been a period where she and Jeannie and I were spending time together, though I don't remember the circumstances. One Halloween, she had invited Jeannie and me to her house—we would meet there, and all go trick-or-treating together. Her room was pink, with a pink canopy bed covered with stuffed animals. Shauna had on a Batgirl costume, Jeannie was Wonder Woman—I remember the sickeningly artificial smell of their plastic masks and capes. I was a princess, wearing one of my mother's old dresses, hiked up around my waist with a belt so I wouldn't trip over it. On my head was a wig of yellow yarn, and a sparkly silver crown I found in the costume aisle of the supermarket when I went with Carmen and Aunt Angela on their big weekly shop. We sat on Shauna's bed, talking about the candy we hoped to get that evening, and the candy our parents had put out for other trick-or-treaters.

Shauna said something about Snickers bars and Baby Ruths, and then she said, *And my brother showed me how to put razors in apples for niggers.* Jeannie was silent. I looked down at my hands, trying to make myself as small as possible. I want to say that Shauna actually showed us how her brother put the razors in those apples. I can almost see her holding one, luridly shiny and red, and slipping the edge of a razor blade through its flesh. I can almost hear the little sucking sound of the apple's skin as she punctures it. I want to say that this is what I remember, but I know, at least I think I know, that it's my imagination, filling in the space where my memory falters out of fear, confusion, shame.

Miriam once told me about a trip she had taken through the South one summer in the 1950s. She was driving down to Florida with a man she was dating at the time, Joe Williams, who was thinking about opening a restaurant there. It was a route her companion had driven before, when he worked as a driver for a rich white man who had a summerhouse in Miami. Somewhere in North Carolina they stopped at a diner to get some food. Joe had suggested this particular place, and said they could get the food to go and have a picnic in a park nearby. He told her that he was tired, and asked her if she wouldn't mind going in and picking up the meal. He had been driving for hours, and Miriam said she was happy to give him a break. As soon as she stepped inside the restaurant, she saw that there were only white people there, a waitress and two men sitting at the counter. Somehow, it hadn't occurred to her that perhaps this was a segregated place—after all, Joe had been there before. She placed her order with the waitress and sat down at the counter to wait for the food. She noticed the men looking her up and down, nudging each other. *What side of the tracks are you from?* one of them asked her. She thought they meant where was she from, so she told them New York. The other man asked her the same question, only this time more slowly, as if she didn't understand English. The waitress came out with her food, eyeing the two men anxiously. Suddenly Miriam understood what they meant. As she was going out the door—the front door—she turned around to them and said, *Well, you have just served a nigger!*

She jumped into the car and told Joe to drive as fast as he could, thinking the men would come after them. She didn't tell him what had happened inside—she didn't want to scare him. *I think I said I had an upset stomach,* she said to me three decades later, laughing and shaking her head as if she still couldn't believe her own audacity. At some point, I'm not sure when, she found out that Joe, a man with dark brown skin, had known all along that it was a "whites only" restaurant, that he had gone there with his employer but had waited in the car while the white man ordered the food. Maybe he had sent Miriam in as a test, to see if she could really pass for white, or maybe as a measure of her courage and devotion to him. Miriam never found out—they split up soon after they got back to New York. They had risked each other's lives, and their own. The violence of segregation and the shame of racism had twisted their relationship into something reckless and false.

Since Miriam told me her story, I've carried it with me, as a kind of talisman against my own fear, my own silence. Miriam spoke out and claimed the truth of who she was: a black woman in her own mind and heart, and a nigger in the eyes of most white people no matter how light her skin was. But that Halloween afternoon at Shauna's, I was speechless. I was so afraid to call attention to myself, to lose the small sense of security I had found in that white neighborhood, and in my white home. I don't think I would have even known what to name myself on that day, with my yellow skin and my straightened hair pinned under a pretend-blond wig. Or what to call my family, how to name my father's

Afro and my Puerto Rican stepmother and my grandfather Luigi's dark skin and "foreign" ways. It was the beginning of many years of silence, of averting my eyes, of receding further and further into myself where there was nothing to explain, nothing to risk.

I SETTLED INTO the rhythms of life in the suburbs, going to school, riding my skateboard with Jeannie in the afternoons, watching *Happy Days* and *Laverne and Shirley* with Marie and Aunt Angela on Saturday nights. Our house was divided into two apartments: I lived upstairs with my father and Carmen. We shared one small bathroom; in the back of the apartment there was a narrow kitchen and a living room that doubled as a dining room into which my father had managed to squeeze both the couch, the table, and a television. My room was next to theirs; it had a twin bed and a chest of drawers and built-in desk, all of white wood. The walls were covered with wallpaper patterned with tiny pink roses. We had to leave my drums behind—there was no space in the house, and the garage only had room for one car. I must have been upset at not being able to bring them with me, but I can't remember now. If I didn't have the photograph of them hidden underneath the bedspread that Christmas I might not believe they were ever mine to begin with. I loved my room, though, because it was mine, and it felt solid, like it would always be mine. At night I'd look out onto the dark street outside my window, amazed at how quiet it was, so different from the 6 train rumbling past my window in the Bronx, or the ambulances wailing up Seventh Avenue outside my window in Harlem.

Downstairs, Gilda and Luigi had their own bedroom off the large kitchen and dining area. Aunt Angela slept on a sofa bed in the living room, and Marie lived in the basement, which had been paneled with wood and fitted with a wet bar, giving it a pseudo-rustic, wintry look, as though it were a lodge in Vermont. It was the perfect room for a teenage girl. My father helped Marie set up her stereo and gave her a new set of speakers. She taped posters all over the walls—the one I remember best was of Elton John as the Pinball Wizard from the film *Tommy*. Off Gilda and Luigi's room was a pink-tiled bathroom, which everybody shared. Luigi always took a long time in there, and in the mornings, when Marie and Aunt Angela were getting ready for school and work, Gilda would go and bang on the door: *Come on, Lou, give someone else a chance!* Although it seemed perfectly normal at the time, I think now this living arrangement must have been uncommon in our new neighborhood, where small bands of nuclear families lived in tidy homes, everyone sleeping in a proper bedroom, and no immigrant grandparents shuffling around in housecoats and robes, calling out to each other in a strange language.

Gilda was up hours before everyone else. She made her coffee, heating the milk in a little enamel pot. She'd go to the deli a few blocks away, where she'd buy *Il Progresso,* the Italian-language newspaper Luigi read every day, and soft, doughy kaiser rolls for breakfast. On Sundays, she'd walk down a steep hill to the Italian bakery. Even in the snow and the rain, she'd make this trip, always by herself. When she got back home, she'd set plates of pastries out on the table: cannoli, éclairs, napoleons, babas—we'd all make our way to her kitchen at some point and take our places around the table, grabbing sections of the Sunday paper. I'd always have milky tea with four teaspoonfuls of sugar and a chocolate éclair. On Sunday evenings, we'd reconvene for dinner, macaroni with gravy and meatballs, and the fresh Italian bread Gilda had brought with the pastries.

Carmen tried to make dinner upstairs on weeknights, but like my father she commuted to the city for work, by the time she got home in the evenings it was already past eight, and she would be too tired to cook. She'd come and kiss me hello, change into her soft pink robe, and go make herself a cup of tea. I'd come out of my room to keep her company, and we'd huddle together under a blanket in front of the television. It was a long way to her job as a secretary at a doctor's office on the Upper East Side—she and my father didn't always drive in together, and often she took the bus into the city, and two subways from there to reach work. At some point my father got a job as a cook in a restaurant near Maplewood. He started late in the morning, driving off in the little gold Celica, and wouldn't get home until midnight.

I'd have dinner downstairs at Gilda's; afterward, I'd go down and listen to records with Marie if she didn't have friends over. She was one of the popular girls in her school—she had lots of friends and always one serious boyfriend. The image of Marie that has stayed with me from that time, that has overridden all others, is of her lying on her bed under the poster of Elton John, talking on the phone. She's in sweatpants and a T-shirt, and she's fingering the "M" pendant on the gold chain that her boyfriend gave her. Maybe she's talking to him on the phone, murmuring softly, or cackling with her best friend Denise. I see myself standing at the foot of the stairs, peering over to her, looking for company. She shouts, *Get out of my room now!* and throws a pillow at me. *Jesus,* I hear her say as I'm going up the stairs, *I can't have any privacy.* Later she comes looking for me upstairs. She hugs me and tells me she's sorry. *Let's have a slumber party,* she says, and I beam with excitement. We grab a tub of chocolate chip ice cream from Gilda's overstuffed freezer and run back down to her room. We sing along to her records, or have a tickling fight. Or I ask her what it's like to kiss a boy, and she tells me all the details. I scrunch up my nose in disgust and say, *No way—I can't believe you do that!*

Sometimes during the summers Aunt Angela would take Marie, Gilda, and me down to the Jersey Shore for the day. We'd pack a cooler full of soda, and Gilda would make us sandwiches, which we'd invariably break into somewhere along the way. We called Aunt Angela's car "the boat" because it was so big and wide. It was a convertible, and we'd ride with the top down, the searing summer air rushing past our faces, the endless promise of the blue sky above us. Marie would sit in the front seat with her mother, and Gilda and I would be in the back. The black vinyl seats were hot and sticky against my legs, and I'd squirm to get comfortable most of the way there. Aunt Angela kept the radio on the oldies station, music from the fifties that she grew up on. She loved all the girl bands, the Ronettes, the Shirelles, the Supremes—whenever they came on she'd turn up the volume and she, Marie, and I would sing, shouting above the roar of the highway: *Please mister postman, look and see, if there's a letter, a letter for me . . .* Gilda would never know the words, but she'd laugh and clap to the music, her white hair blowing in the wind.

Luigi had begun his garden soon after we moved. He planted tomatoes, cucumbers, eggplants, zucchini, basil, and oregano along the outer edges of the yard. There was a space behind the garage where he built a kind of trellis out of discarded wood. He planted grapes there, sure that in a couple of years' time he would be able to make his own wine.

He was already in his seventies, ill with diabetes and stiff with arthritis, but he went outside each morning, once the ground had softened after the long, icy winter, and transformed our small backyard into a lush, green little world. By growing the foods of his youth, he changed the very nature of that suburban soil, made it Italian soil, a piece of home. Luigi tended his plants with the hands of a lover, gently and patiently. And he guarded them like a soldier, yelling from his lawn chair in the middle of the yard anytime anyone got too close. Gardening was a man's occupation, being outside with your hands in the earth, knowing what to plant at what time by the season and the phases of the moon, while the women worked inside, in the space of the home. How different he was, sweating in his white undershirt with his makeshift tools, from our middle-class neighbors who rarely spoke to him, women with special gardening shoes and wide-brimmed hats to keep their delicate skin safe from the sun. For Luigi, gardening was no genteel pastime; it was about putting extra food on the table, being useful in old age, taking care of his family in the isolation of the suburbs, so far away from the rest of the family in the Bronx, impossibly far from Carolei.

After Luigi had coaxed his vegetables from the soil, Gilda would turn them into food for the table. She cut the cucumbers and tomatoes into salads, seasoned with olive oil and salt. The zucchini she fried with garlic; she baked eggplant with tomato sauce and cheese. Along the side of the house, Luigi had planted a row of rosebushes, just for Gilda. They rarely seemed to bloom, but every once in a while Gilda would clip one and put it in a small vase by the window over the sink, a place where she spent much of her time. She'd point it out to anyone who came into the kitchen: *Look, my rose came!* The grapes were another matter. The birds ate the first buds, after that nothing new ever grew. Like ghosts, the dried vines clung to the walls and roof of the garage with long, withered fingers.

Sometimes when there were no cars in the garage I'd go in and sit on an old rocking chair that was stored in one of the corners. I had discovered Judy Blume books, which I would only read in private—because of their stories about girls getting their periods and boys growing pubic hair, I was embarrassed at the thought of my father or Gilda seeing me with them. Inside the garage it was a dusty, cobwebby white. There were small windows along its two side walls, and Luigi's grapevines twined across them, blocking out much of the light. The ceiling, I found out only recently, was covered with asbestos. The garage was filled with a dank, earthen smell, even though the floor was concrete, and the smell of wet newspaper. I would slide under the garage door, which was always partially open, and pull the chair against one of the walls beneath the window. I loved sitting in the diffuse light of that space, watching how the light seeped in through the windows and under the door. I could see Luigi's feet as he crossed the driveway during his daily gardening. He always wore the same black shoes, which he shined with thick black polish and buffed with an old dishrag. "Black Shoe" was my nickname for him, although I never called him that to his face. It was comforting to watch those shoes pass back and forth, signs of life in the world outside, of my family inside the house, even as I cloistered myself away, even as I hid from them.

One day I found a baby bird that had fallen from the tree in front of our house. It was still alive, but one of its wings was broken, hanging dejectedly at its side. I scooped the bird up and brought it into the garage, where I put it into a small wooden crate stuffed with newspaper. I kept the bird hidden in a corner for a few days, sneaking out to feed it milk from a dropper and tiny pieces of toast with butter. The bird would look up at me as I dropped the milk into its feebly opened beak, its eyes glazed, its head wobbling. I had never held a bird before. I could feel its heart beating when I stroked its feathers, a faint fluttering as if there were tiny wings deep inside its body. Each night I would pray to God to make the little bird fly again, but the next morning it just seemed weaker. When it died I sat in the garage and wept over its stiff brown body. Luigi heard me and raised the garage door. *What's a matter for you?* he asked. I pointed at the cage. He peered in. *E morte? Dead,* I nodded. He came over and patted me on the head. *No you cry, Papano.* He took me into the backyard, to the wild brambles that grew behind the clothesline, and helped me dig a small grave. Afterward, he put his hands together and gestured toward me with his chin to say a prayer. When we were done, I saw that Gilda had been watching from the window. She smiled and waved at me. There was a cup of tea waiting for me on the table, milky and sweet, when I came back into the house. *You did a good thing,* she said. *Now he's in heaven.*

A YEAR AFTER we moved, my father and Carmen split up. He had been coming home later and later each night. Carmen wouldn't come with me when I went down to Gilda's apartment—she'd say she had housework to catch up on. When my father was around he seemed remote, wraithlike. I remember how vacant his eyes looked when I told him about school or what I'd done that day—it was as if he had stopped listening long ago. On the rare nights the three of us ate together, he would drum his hands on the table, looking off into the distance and humming wildly and loudly to music only he could hear. I was afraid he was going crazy, but now I know that it was heroin. I've never understood why he suddenly seemed so much worse than he had been in the years before. Maybe it was the pressure of starting life over in a new place, far from anything that was familiar. The commuting, the mortgage payments, Carmen's dream of having a child of her own—the

American Dream wasn't enough for him, or perhaps it was too much. Heroin, the great constant in his life since he came back from the war, became an escape from his suburban escape.

Late at night I'd listen to my father and Carmen shouting at each other through the wall between our bedrooms, her voice rising and his fading. I couldn't imagine then how lonely it must have been for Carmen, losing her husband to drugs, living so far from her friends and her mother, in a neighborhood where she knew no one, in a house where she didn't always feel welcome. There were no other Latinos I knew of in the neighborhood, and for a young, urban woman—she wasn't yet thirty—there was nothing to do outside the space of the home. She and Aunt Angela always seemed too busy to spend much time together. Her relationship with Gilda and Luigi hadn't warmed—I never saw them fighting, but Carmen told me later that the three of them never got along. *Gilda was so subservient, it made me really angry,* she said. *She used to put your grandfather's slippers on his feet every morning. Why couldn't he do it himself?* I wonder now if they never got used to having a Puerto Rican daughter-in-law. They had left East Harlem for the Bronx to escape the growing number of Puerto Rican immigrants—*They're taking over the neighborhood* was a refrain Carmen knew all too well. Now they had made it all the way to the suburbs, to a nice white neighborhood, and here was one living under their own roof. Maybe living together couldn't make us all into a family, as my father says he had hoped. It certainly hadn't brought Carmen and my grandparents together; instead it seemed to reopen old wounds that were both personal and communal.

They were able to lay their differences down at least once. The town of Maplewood had its own community pool, where Jeannie and the other kids in my class all went most days during summer vacation. I went there with Jeannie for the first time at the end of

May, a sticky, hazy morning, when the pool had just opened for the season, with a new bathing suit and Carmen's big beach towel rolled up in a plastic bag. When we got to the gate, the security guard wouldn't let me in. *You, okay,* he said to Jeannie. *But she's not a member.* I looked through the thick iron gate at all the kids, white kids, splashing around in the bright blue pool. Our family had been living in Maplewood for more than a year, but apparently there had been something wrong with our membership application when Aunt Angela took it in to the office. Carmen told me many years later that it was me they didn't want in the pool, that they had made up all sorts of excuses not to accept the whole family because they didn't allow black people. Once she and Gilda and Aunt Angela realized what was really going on, they went down to the pool themselves. *You should have seen us—we raised hell that day,* Carmen said. I picture them now, three ethnic furies storming past the pool's iron gate and into the manager's office. Their skin was light enough to get them through that gate, and they weren't going to leave me behind.

Before she left, Carmen told me that I could call her whenever I needed her, that if things got really bad in the house, meaning my father, she would come and get me. We were sitting together on my bed. Her things were in boxes in the hallway; some of her friends were going to drive her back to the Bronx. We were both crying—she kept blowing her nose with a handkerchief dotted with little red hearts.

For a few months afterward, my father was home more. He'd make dinner for me, help me with my homework. I'd watch him clean the house, his back to me as he vacuumed and washed the dishes. *There, nice and clean,* he'd say cheerfully when he'd turn around and notice me standing there. Some nights he'd invite me up into the attic, which he had turned into a kind of den, where he listened to his jazz records and played his vibraphone. I'd sit on the beanbag chair he'd bought just for that space. I didn't like that chair—I could feel myself sinking into it as though it were going to swallow me whole. He'd sit across from me in his old leather reclining chair, his head leaned back, his eyes closed. After while I'd slip downstairs to my room—he never seemed to look up in time to see me go.

With Carmen gone there was one less income in the house. My father kept getting jobs in different restaurants in the area, never staying in one place longer than a few months. I know now that he was fired, for not showing up, maybe, or being high on the job. He'd never use the word "fired"—instead he'd say, *Oh, I'm not working there anymore.* I'd hear him fighting sometimes with Gilda and Aunt Angela—the front door would slam, and he'd drive off somewhere. Luigi's health was beginning to fail—he'd shuffle around the house in his robe and slippers, moaning and cursing, and he slept later and later each day. There were piles of medical bills on the kitchen counter downstairs. Aunt Angela had found a job as a secretary with a construction company soon after we had moved—now she and Gilda started working together on Saturdays, cleaning the rich people's houses on the other side of town. Marie had just turned sixteen and had her driver's license. She worked after school, and saved up enough money to buy herself a used car. She'd come home late a lot of the time, or stay over at her girlfriends.'

I GOT A new ten-speed bike on our second Christmas in the new house. Everyone in the family had saved up to buy it for me. It was a silvery blue with low handlebars that curved down, nothing like the old banana-seated three-speed with the faulty breaks that

Marie and I had shared in the Bronx—we'd weave through the traffic on East Tremont Avenue, Marie on the seat, me squeezed precariously between the high handlebars. In Maplewood I'd ride my new bike for hours, sailing down the many hills, my whole existence the pavement beneath my wheels and the wide sky above my head. The first time I rode without holding on to the handlebars I felt like I had conquered the world. I used to watch out my window as the neighborhood boys rode by my street in the evenings after dinner, their hands resting on their thighs as they pedaled. It was hard to figure out just by looking how they kept their bikes straight, the thin wheels hugging the street. So I practiced, riding back and forth along Boyden Avenue, lifting my hands for a few seconds at a time off the handlebars. One day I just sat up on the seat and kept pedaling, my arms crossed against my flat chest, and I rode a smooth, even line for two blocks. From that point on, I'd ride almost everywhere this way, though few other girls did, except Jeannie. On weekends she would meet me in front of my house on her bike, and we'd ride to Irvington, the neighboring town, for pizza. We'd take the long way home, cruising down the side streets from one town to the other, talking about school and our favorite teen idols. Whenever we started to go downhill, we'd pedal as fast as we could and then glide the rest of the way, laughing and waving our hands above our heads.

Jeannie and I never talked about our families, except to giggle about Black Shoe's loud voice or to complain about how annoying her little sister could be. Instead, we started getting into trouble. We'd smoke still-burning cigarette butts that we found on the sidewalks, oblivious to the lips that had touched them first, choking as the stale smoke hit our lungs. Once we bought punks and sparklers in the school playground from a sixth-grader—we set them off in the driveway until Gilda came out yelling and shaking her broom at us. *What are you trying to do, set my house on fire?* Soon after we began stealing together.

It all started with earrings. On Saturday afternoons when she was finished working, Aunt Angela would drop Jeannie and me off at the Livingston Mall. The two of us would wander in and out of the stores, gawking at lava lamps and black light posters, flipping through records. One day we went into a new jewelry store. I had had my ears pierced for my twelfth birthday. Marie had taken me and held my hand as the young woman at the jewelry counter stamped my earlobes with something that looked like a laser gun. After a shock of bright pain, it was over, and I had new posts of burnished gold. Getting my ears pierced had been my only acquiescence to femininity. Although I wouldn't have been able to articulate it then, having the gold in my ears made me feel "Italian," and so part of my father's family. Gold was what you got for birthdays, for graduations, for anniversaries; it was a rite of passage. The delicate gold earrings of black-eyed little girls, teenage boys' gold rope chains with crosses hanging from them just so, gold watches glinting at the wrists of *men of honor*—gold meant belonging. In the evening after I had my ears pierced, Marie showed me how to clean around the posts with a cotton swab soaked in hydrogen peroxide. *Keep twisting the posts every day, it helps the holes heal,* she told me as she dabbed at my red, swollen earlobes. *In a couple of months, I'll let you wear my hoops.*

That day at the mall, Jeannie looked at me and said, *I dare you to steal a pair of earrings.* There were rows of them hanging from plastic holders on wooden displays along the countertop: gold studs and hoops of all different sizes and thicknesses, jingly silver earrings shaped like teardrops, inlaid with fake diamonds and turquoise. I grabbed a pair of small gold hoops that were twisted like ram's horns, and shoved them into my jeans pocket. Jeannie took a pair as well, and we walked quickly out of the store, without looking back. We grinned at each other as we waited in the parking lot for Aunt Angela to pick us up. I don't remember what we said to each other, if we said anything at all. I only remember the feeling of the earrings in my pocket, their surprising weight and the cool, raised surface of the twisted metal. From then on, Jeannie and I would steal earrings from all sorts of places, and we never got caught. I must have had a hundred pairs stuffed into the corners of my underwear drawer.

After school, we'd go to the Stop N Shop supermarket down the road and take colored pens, packages of pencils, and pink gum erasers, slipping them under our shirts. I'm not sure why we stole school supplies—they were much less interesting than sparkly jewelry. Every night for the past year I had written in a diary, and I'd draw in it with the markers and crayons I took, hearts and unicorns and castles surrounded by stars. I had never kept a diary until I found an old, moldy book lying on the sidewalk near some garbage bags on one of my bike rides. It was a girl's diary, faded pink cloth on the outside, pages of sloping handwriting on water-stained, gold-lined paper inside. There was no name on the diary, but a date, 1954. The girl who wrote it mostly talked about her boyfriend, how he wanted to go all the way—I knew what this meant now from the Judy Blume books—she had held him off for as long as she could until one night in his car she said yes. After that some of the pages were torn out—I never found out what it had been like for her, whether she had enjoyed it. The rest of the pages were filled with descriptions of fights the girl had with her mother, *that bitch*. The boyfriend was never mentioned again. I felt strange having something so personal, reading another girl's secret words, so I threw it out. A few weeks later I bought my own diary.

The odd thing is that I don't remember what I wrote about—if I dared to describe the sense of disintegration I felt at home, or of missing Miriam, whom I saw only on holidays, or my mother, far away in Italy. Other than the drawings I made, I only remember that I practiced my handwriting. Before, I had written in large, blocky, childish letters, and at some point I consciously decided to write in a more mature way. I'd spend hours alone in my room, learning to write in grown-up cursive like the girl in the old diary. I can still see those pages in my own diary, line after line of sweeping, looping capital *I*'s.

One day after Jeannie and I had left the Stop N Shop with our usual hoard, a man stopped us in the parking lot. *Give me back that stuff,* he grumbled, holding out his hand. *What stuff?* Jeannie said, crossing her arms around the lumps of stolen items underneath her shirt. *We don't have anything,* I said. The man told us that he was the store detective, that he had been watching us on the surveillance camera for the past couple of weeks. Sheepishly, we pulled out the pens and markers and handed them over. The man made us wait there for a what seemed forever, telling us that he was trying to decide whether to call our parents or send us straight to jail. I realize now he was probably only trying to scare us, but we believed him about going to jail. I looked over at Jeannie. She was completely still, and there were tears rolling down her cheeks. I begged the man to let us go, making up all kinds of stories about how we were in a gang and we were forced to steal as an initiation. I couldn't believe that Jeannie, who was so often the instigator of these little adventures, wouldn't speak up for us.

The man never called my house, but soon after I got into an ugly fight with Gilda. She liked Marie's friends, especially Denise, who was also Italian American and whose family had come to Maplewood from Brooklyn years before. Whenever Denise visited, Gilda would always tell her how pretty she looked and ask after her parents. When Jeannie came over, Gilda said very little, telling us only to make ourselves some sandwiches and leaving the room. One afternoon, when Gilda had been particularly indifferent to Jeannie, I heard her talking on the phone to Denise, telling her Marie wasn't home. Gilda was giggling like a teenager at something Denise had said, and before she hung up she said, *Come visit soon, honey—I miss you over here.*

There was a certain distance between Gilda and me that never seemed to close, an almost imperceptible formality that I could sense but never quite name or understand. I felt often that I was more a guest in the house than part of the family. I would think twice about looking in Gilda's refrigerator, and always ask whether I could get a drink or have a cookie. I don't know how much of this was my own lack of belief that I really belonged there, and how much was Gilda's sometimes gruff, awkward way with me. On Sunday evenings she, Aunt Angela, and Marie would play cards at the kitchen table, their cans of soda at their sides, a pile of pennies and nickels in front of each of them. I'd sit with them, watching as they played poker and gin, betting their pennies and fake-cheating, peeking over at each other's cards and laughing as they shooed each other away. Gilda would seem so happy and comfortable, so sure of herself with them. I'd chime in to try to make them laugh, tell them my silly kid jokes: *Why did the monkey fall out of the tree? Because it was dead!* Aunt Angela and Marie would groan, and Gilda would smile confusedly. *What she means, the monkey's dead?*

Aunt Angela and Marie looked so much alike, the same short feathered hair, the clothes they shared because they were the same size, even the way they smoked their cigarettes was similar—the deep drags, the long, slow exhales. I'd look into each of their faces, my aunt, my cousin, my grandmother, wondering which of their features I might have inherited, wondering if anyone would ever tell me how much I looked like them. At these moments I felt like I had just come into a story that had begun long ago without me. It seemed as if the three of them had had an entire lifetime of jokes, games, secrets, and tears before I came along. I didn't know how to catch up. Then Aunt Angela would invite me to play a round with them, explaining the rules and handing me some coins from her own pot. I'd follow along, excited if I had been dealt something good, holding up my cards proudly for them to see. *Flush!* I'd call out. *Do I win this hand?*

After Gilda hung up with Denise that day, I lay into her with all the fury my eleven-year-old self could muster. *Why do you only like Marie's friends but you hate my friends? I think you hate me, too!* I shrieked. Before she could answer, I ran out of the room. Later Aunt Angela called me downstairs. She and Gilda were standing in the kitchen. Aunt Angela's eyes flashed with blue-flame fire. *Don't you ever talk to your grandmother like that again, do you understand me?* She nudged me over toward Gilda. *Now you apologize.* I told her I was sorry, but I couldn't look her in the eye. *It's okay,* Gilda said, *let's forget it.*

But I couldn't forget it. I didn't feel better because I had exposed a problem that we might be able to work out together. It was just my own small explosion—it didn't mean that anything was really out in the open. Instead, I was worried that I'd get sent away, that this was the final proof the family needed that I didn't belong with them. I sulked in my room until my father burst through my door late that night. He had just come home from work, but he must have already spoken to Aunt Angela. *How dare you talk to your grandmother that way, she does everything for you,* he yelled. He tore the belt from his pants and began beating me on the behind with it until I screamed for him to stop. He stormed out as suddenly as he had come in, leaving me crying on the floor. No one on either side of my family had ever given me a whipping before. My back and my behind burned—when I checked the next morning bruises had bloomed across my skin like black roses.

JUST AFTER MY twelfth birthday I got my first period. I woke up one morning to find my pajamas and sheets covered with blood. I knew what it was—I had seen the sex-education films in school, we girls in our classroom watching one version of the story of puberty, the boys lined up on folding chairs in the gym watching another. We learned about the wonderful changes our bodies would go through, the glories of being a woman, what happened when a man and a woman loved each other and got married and wanted to make a baby. Jeannie and I rolled our eyes through the whole excruciating fifty minutes, and doodled in our notebooks when the school nurse turned on the lights and asked if there were any questions. I never understood why we couldn't all get the same information at the same time—I didn't believe then that boys and girls were so different from each other. Over the past couple of years I had begun to feel more like a boy anyway. I hated wearing dresses and thought makeup was stupid. What girls my age did for fun was a mystery to me—all I wanted to do was ride my bike or my skateboard and listen to Led Zeppelin records. Also a mystery was my own sexuality—I had crushes on boys in my class, boys named Vinny and Nicky and Vito, but they didn't look twice at me. And I'm not sure if it was those boys' attention I wanted, or their power. The free way they had with their bodies, how they didn't seem to be burdened by anything. *Yeah, whatever,* I'd hear them say coolly to each other. I wanted that "whatever" for myself.

I knew about menstruation—I just wasn't expecting it to happen to me. The signs were already there, the pimples on my forehead, the small bumps that were pushing out of my chest, so smooth just a few months before. But I ignored these changes, hoping they'd just go away. Some of the other girls at school talked about how excited they were to get their periods, how their mothers had already bought them their first boxes of sanitary napkins, just in case. That morning, I rushed to the bathroom to rinse out my pajamas. I rolled up a wad of toilet paper to soak up the blood that was now running down my thighs. I felt like I was going to be sick. My father was still in bed—I had planned to take the sheets downstairs to the washing machine before he woke up and saw them. But when I came out of the bathroom, he was standing in the doorway of my room, looking worried. *Let's go downstairs,* he said nervously, and took me to the pink bathroom. Aunt Angela and Marie were rushing to get ready for work and school, blow-drying their hair, putting on each other's mascara and blue eye shadow. My father mumbled something to them and went back upstairs. *I can't do it, I'm late,* Marie said, glancing over at me. *Ma, please, you take care of it.* I sat on the toilet, my cheeks burning with shame. Aunt Angela took down a box of Kotex from the mirrored cabinet against the wall. She pulled one out, monstrously thick and white, and showed me how to stick it onto my underwear. Before she rushed out the door she hugged me. *Congratulations, babe, you're a woman now.*

A few months later, on a sleepy Saturday afternoon, I was reading in my room. I could hear loud noises coming from downstairs, banging and muffled shouts. Gilda and Aunt Angela had gone shopping, and Marie was out with her boyfriend. Earlier that morning, my father and Luigi were outside working in the garden—a rare occasion of them spending time together at all—but when I crept down to see what was happening, I found them both in the kitchen, yelling at each other. Luigi was cursing my father in Calabrese, telling him to go to the devil. It was summertime, a particularly hot and humid day, and the windows and back door of the downstairs kitchen were all thrown open, light pouring in from every direction. Suddenly I realized that my father was holding a butcher knife. His back was toward me—his hair was long and wild, and he was drenched in sweat. I saw him raise the knife over his head and rush toward Luigi, swearing that he'd kill him. *Vai, uccidame,* Luigi said, ramming himself against my father like a bull. Go ahead, kill me. I dare you. I stood frozen in the doorway. And then I started to scream.

What happened next is a blur. I see my father's wild eyes, the knife dropping to the floor. Luigi standing alone in the kitchen, disheveled and shaking. I left Maplewood soon after that. Miriam found out—I don't know how. Despite how uncertain I felt about my place in my father's family, my life was there now. I had been uprooted twice before, and I didn't want to give up the tenuous hold I had found in my new home. When I asked Miriam later she told me that she and Gilda had spoken over the phone many times during the weeks after the fight, trying to decide what was best for me— should I stay in Maplewood, with Carmen gone and my father in such turmoil, or should I go back to Harlem and live with Miriam again? This was the beginning of their tentative, long-distance friendship. It continued for the rest of their lives, through holiday phone calls, condolence cards, and birthday gifts sent back and forth through me. Miriam said it had been my mother who made the final decision, that she had come back from Italy to set me up in school in New York as soon as she found out what had happened between my father and Luigi.

It must have been August when I left the house on Boyden

Avenue. I've forgotten everything that happened after that day in the kitchen, as if there's a brick wall where those memories are supposed to be. Was I afraid of my father? Did I keep away from him, closing the door to my room and turning up my radio whenever he came home? Was he the one who told me I was moving back with Miriam? I don't remember packing my bags, or the sight of my empty room. I have only an image of me standing at the back door of the kitchen, saying goodbye to Aunt Angela and Gilda. They're both hugging me, both crying. *You be good,* Gilda sniffles. Aunt Angela says, *You always have a home with us—don't ever forget it.* Don't ever forget. It's like another one of those snapshots that was never taken, a moment no one ever documented, no one ever witnessed. Now it lives only in my mind, the memory fading so that soon even I will doubt that it really happened, that the life I had there with them ever happened at all.

CHAPTER NINE

Miriam finally left Harlem in the summer of 1978. During her last few years there, she had devoted most of her time to the work of historical preservation. She had given up her job in public housing, disheartened that she couldn't make a difference in how low-income apartments were built and maintained. I asked her once if it had been hard to leave that work behind after so many years. *The projects and the tenements—they'll never be anything but prisons,* she said. *What more could I do?* She had always pointed out to me certain buildings in Harlem that were in danger of being torn down or burned down—*This is where Langston lived and wrote his poems, this is where people used to do the Lindy Hop during the war.* Through her organization, the Emanuel Pieterson Historical Society, she was able to get some of those buildings cleaned up, with bronze plaques by their doors that explained what happened there. *People have to know how great Harlem was, and what it still could be,* she'd say. I wonder now what she'd think about the new gentrification of Harlem, the wealthy white people buying up blocks of brownstones, some of which she might have helped preserve and restore.

I've found little information on the Emanuel Pieterson Historical Society. But looking in an old issue of the *Amsterdam News,*
where Miriam had once worked, I found an article dated January
6, 1951, describing plans the New York City government was
undertaking to build a series of air raid shelters in case of nuclear
attack. The article described five immense underground shelters,
with room for over twenty-five thousand people in each of them,
all equipped with hospitals, cafeterias, and sleeping quarters
designed for prolonged use. The proposed shelters would all be
built in Manhattan, but none in Harlem. Miriam would have
arrived in Harlem a couple of years after this article was published. I wonder if construction was ever begun on any of these
bunkers, which would have been like small neighborhoods underground. Did she know about them? I can imagine her on yet
another picket line in front of City Hall, a homemade sign in her
hand, shouting, *A-bomb shelter for Harlem!* Miriam spent her whole
adult life, all the time she lived in Harlem, fighting for shelter,
fighting for home. She did everything in her power to see that
black people lived in clean, safe, affordable places. That Harlem
itself could be a haven where black lives were precious. And in her
apartment at 1809 Seventh Avenue, she tried to build a home for
herself, for my mother, for me.

It was time to go, she said of her move to the apartment downtown that my mother and her boyfriend Paolo had offered her. It
was a small, dark one-bedroom; the windows faced out onto the
back wall of another building. But it would be home for the next
twenty years, the place where Miriam would die. My mother came
back to New York in the mid-1980s. She and Paolo split up—in
time she married someone else, a white nightclub owner from
New York. Miriam and I were the bridesmaids at her wedding. My
mother wore a dress of white leather trimmed with gold. During

the exchanging of the vows, I noticed tears falling from the corners of her eyes. It was the first time I had ever seen my mother cry. After I left Maplewood, I came to live in the apartment with Miriam, sleeping on a single bed in the living room. I would end up spending the rest of my school years back at Sacred Heart.

The year I turned thirteen, I found a record in a used bin at a flea market, *Germ Free Adolescents* by X Ray Spex. They were a punk band—it was the loudest music I had ever heard, even louder than when I played my drums to beat the train on Westchester Square. Poly Styrene, the lead singer, wore white go-go boots and silver lamé dresses. She was biracial like me, with the same springy corkscrew hair and the same in-between skin. She sang about the bewildering aspects of identity, the feeling of freakishness and ugliness that made you want to smash the mirror when you looked into it. But Poly Styrene was no victim. She made it seem cool to be an outsider, to not fit in. The next day, I cut off most of my hair, which was growing out from the last time it was straightened. I dyed the unruly virgin roots hot pink and peacock blue. Music became a kind of home for me, especially punk and the glam rock of the early 1970s. It was music made by people who didn't belong anywhere, people who were in between: black and white, male and female. In high school I even won a prize for an essay I wrote about the cover of David Bowie's album *Space Oddity*. With my dyed hair, my thrift-shop dresses and combat boots, and the safety pins in my ears, I found a way to feel comfortable in my own skin. To stand out because I wanted to, to highlight my difference instead of trying to fade into the background, gave me a freedom I had never known. For once, I had stopped being the good girl, the one who smiled and apologized and tiptoed on little mouse-feet. For once, for a while, I had found a new tribe, and I felt that I had nothing left to prove.

A few times a month, I would visit my family in New Jersey. I still saw them every Christmas, Easter, and Thanksgiving, still had the double feasts between Gilda's table and Miriam's. My father had moved back to New York not long after I had left, and sometimes the two of us would ride up for the day on the bus. The second floor—our old apartment—had been rented out to tenants to bring in extra cash to pay the mortgage bills. The tenants had a little girl, and now my room was hers. Whenever I stayed over, I'd sleep with Aunt Angela on the sofa bed. In 1993, Aunt Angela died in that bed. Although she had already been through menopause, she had started to bleed again. For months she said nothing, thinking it would just go away. It turned out to be cervical cancer—sixteen months later, she was gone. For a year afterward, I dreamed of her, the same dream all the time. She'd sit at the foot of my bed and say, *Don't worry, babe—you'll see, it all works out.* Then she'd smile at me and disappear. The dreams stopped when the year was over.

My grandfather Luigi died when I was in the tenth grade. His funeral was in the Bronx, the pews in the chapel filled with ancient-looking Italian men and women who came to pay their respects. It seemed that there were no young people there except Marie and me, and everyone spoke in Calabrese, even my father, who greeted aunts and uncles and his parents' *paesani* who had moved to the Bronx from East Harlem over the years. After the move to New Jersey, my family had rarely visited the Bronx, and no one from there ever made the trip out to Maplewood. The journey, physically and metaphorically, had been too far. When Luigi was being interred, Gilda wailed and sobbed, her arms outstretched, her bony fingers clawing at the air—*Please don't leave me, Lou. Don't leave me here alone.* My father held her, tears streaming down his own face. Gilda's grief terrified me—a lamentation so elemental, so ancient, so powerful it seemed to shake the ground we were standing on. I was afraid because I knew that I had the capacity for that kind of sorrow, that it would be my inheritance from Gilda. It ran through my blood, which was also her blood.

Sometime after Luigi died, the neighbors next door to the house in Maplewood moved out. They had been the only people in the neighborhood to greet us when our family moved in, the only people Gilda was close to outside the family. She would babysit their kids, and bring them batches of cookies and vegetables from the garden. I sat with her on the porch and together we watched the moving van come and take their boxes and furniture away. Gilda wrung her hands and sighed. *The new neighbors, I just don't know,* she said. *What about them, Grandma?* I asked. *What's wrong?* She looked from my face to the large, empty house outside the window. *I hope they're white,* she said. She said the words to me, speaking to me, but not really seeing me. Once again, I said nothing. What was there to say after all these years? Where would I even begin? We sat together in silence, watching the movers, and I raged inside. I raged mostly because I loved her. And because I understood that her love for me could only ever be partial, a love based on an almost acrobatic capacity for contradiction and denial.

In 1989 I watched as the horror of Yusef Hawkins's murder played itself out on the evening news. Hawkins had been a young black man who had come to Bensonhurst, an Italian American neighborhood in Brooklyn, one evening with some of his friends, looking to buy a used car. He was attacked by a mob of local boys—thirty boys armed with baseball bats, one of them with a gun. Hawkins was shot to death, the boys scattered. No one said who it was who pulled the trigger. There was speculation that a neighborhood girl had been dating a black man and the killers mistook Hawkins for him. Afterward, African American protesters marched through Bensonhurst, demanding justice. News crews descended upon the scene in a frenzy of anticipation over what might happen between the marchers and the neighborhood spectators. And as the marchers walked peacefully and solemnly through the streets, many carrying lit candles whose small flames wavered and sputtered, groups of Italian American men, women, and children jeered at them, telling them to go back where they came from. Old ladies hooted and cursed from out their windows. Large men threw watermelons as the black men, women, and children passed by, the fruit splattering red at their feet. Watermelon, a fruit beloved in Sicily, became a weapon Italian American hecklers used against their perceived enemies—clearly, tragically, the irony was lost on them. Reporters interviewed bystanders who said, *We just want them out of the neighborhood—our boys were only protecting our homes.* I watched these images with a feeling of nausea that stayed with me for weeks afterward. The jeering spectators, their faces twisted with murderous hatred, looked like people in my own family. The women hissing from their windows looked like Gilda. This was the story of my father's family and my mother's family writ large, and in blood. The policed borders of the body and the community, the illicit desire, the ancient rules broken, and the brutal consequences of such transgressions. It was my history, but I survived it. Yusef Hawkins wasn't so fortunate.

Gilda's new neighbors weren't white. They were an African American family: two parents, two kids, two cars, and a dog, just like the white family before them. Over the following years, Gilda grew friendly with them, little by little at first, until finally she was closer to them than she was to the original neighbors. Not long before she died, the African American neighbors also moved out, along with many of the other families in the area. There had been a string of robberies along Boyden Avenue. Marie found a bullet lodged near the door to the porch, the door where Gilda would always stand, waiting for her children and grandchildren to come home, waving as we pulled up into the driveway or walked from the bus stop. *It's those kids from Newark,* my father said, *they've been coming over here from across Irvington Avenue.* He blamed the trouble on crack.

DURING MY FIRST year of film school, I decided to make a short documentary about my father. I wanted to focus on the life he led in the kitchen, of his love for cooking and eating. The shoot took place on a late summer day at the house in Maplewood. I asked my father to make baked ziti, his specialty, the recipe passed on to him by his grandmother Luisa. My father is the master of the dish. He makes it every Christmas and Easter, and for birthdays and other celebrations. Usually he cooks alone, making enough to feed an army. He'll give me a huge tin of fresh macaroni, plus a few containers frozen and extra gravy, just in case. During the shoot, Gilda and my father's girlfriend Susan sat at the kitchen table, watching my father chop and mix and stir. I followed him with the camera as he went through the preparation step by step, and I followed Susan and my grandmother moving through the periphery, sometimes trying to help, but mostly just praising my father—*Oh, that smells delicious*—acting as his captive audience.

Sometimes I watch the videotape from that day—it never became the documentary I had planned, but remains raw footage, never digested into narrative. The footage is degraded now, pixels dropping here and there. The camerawork is shaky, the images are blown out so that all the white objects in the frame take over, bleeding into everything else. I am two people in this narrative: the graduate student beginning a documentary about my father that I will never finish, and the me of many years after. The me that watches the images on the screen, receiving them from my younger, hopeful self.

I see now how clumsy I was with the video camera, how I forgot to check the iris so that everything looks too bright, the light coming in from the kitchen windows, the reflection of the knife as my father chops onions and garlic, the mozzarella resting soft and exposed as flesh on the wooden cutting board. Everything glows with some otherworldly light—the kitchen looks like heaven, a room filled with ghosts and those who are becoming ghosts right before my eyes.

Ghosts: my Grandfather Luigi at the head of the table by the wall, drinking espresso and cracking almonds with his old nutcracker, dead twenty years ago. My Aunt Angela on the inside of the table by the door, drinking her Pepsi and smoking her Parliament cigarette, gone ten years after her father. The ghosts of myself and my cousin Marie as kids, impatient then to leave the table. To leave the table, to leave this life behind and have no idea how much we will miss it one day.

Through the lens I watch what's left of this family, which is my own family, go through the motions of an ancient ritual, preparing the feast day meal. This meal that would have been prepared for at least thirty people before we moved to the suburbs and dissipated. Back in the Bronx. Or East Harlem. Or in the hills of Calabria and Sicily where our old ones were born.

I pan around the space of the kitchen and dining area with my camera-eye, my camera-heart. Across the wood-paneled walls, the linoleum floor. The black and white TV on the counter, beneath it the cabinets that hold pots and pans and lentils and cookies. The old brand names: Progresso, Ronzoni, Contadina, Polly-O. The wooden dining table that welcomes and waits. The windows behind the table. Flood of light. I see myself as a child sitting at that table, dunking biscotti into tea, watching Gilda fry meatballs at the old stove, a pot of sauce simmering on the back burner, and all the smells filling this warm space flooded with light. Out the window to the wild backyard which was once Luigi's garden. Past the dry, tangled grapevines whose meager fruit was eaten by birds. Past the memories of eggplant, tomato, zucchini.

I zoom in as my father fries the tomato paste. Susan is behind him, saying how good it smells. *That's just the beginning,* my father says, and beams. He is so proud of his ability to make magic from food, his special gift. Gilda wanders in and out of the frame, tidying up in the kitchen. Always cleaning. When the rest of the tomatoes are in the pot and the sauce is starting to bubble, to become, she will come by every few minutes with her dishcloth and wipe the tiny red splashes from the stovetop.

June, when you gonna put the meat in? Gilda has always called my father June, short for Junior, Luigi Junior. Marie calls him Uncle Junior, and his friends call him JR. After an early childhood of not quite knowing what to call him myself, I have long settled on Dad. So many names, so many layers of claiming, of kinship. *Now, Ma.* He ruffles a little at his mother's attempted intervention and slides browned pork ribs, then fried meatballs, from the battered cast-iron pan into the sauce. Susan gestures toward me. *JR, tell your daughter about your toys when you were little. Wow,* he sighs, *I almost forgot about that—that's right, honey, I had a little cooking set, my own pots and pans, even then. Remember, Ma?* Gilda turns to me. *I remember. He didn't want to play with nothing else, only the little pots. And he's still the same!*

I focus on my father's hands stirring the béchamel. He has always been slight—thin and wiry—even in times of relative good health. His hands seem to belong to someone else, large and broad, with thick fingers. A worker's hands, like his father's.

Unmistakable markers of masculinity that betray how soft and delicate he is. He stirs the dense mixture of ricotta and egg that will bind the macaroni together. *Can I lick the spoon?* I ask, knowing he'll caution me on the dangers of ingesting raw egg, my response to him always the same: *For me, it's safe.*

I pan the camera a little clumsily to the sink as he drains the macaroni. Again the blinding light of enamel, pasta, and rising steam. Gilda calls from the edge of the frame: *June, did you sign the papers yet?* The business of the house, from which I've always been removed. The baby of the family, the outsider looking in. *Not now, Ma, let's talk about it after dinner.* I follow behind, adjust the lens. Always chasing after partial meanings.

My father relates to me as if I were still a little girl. He even speaks to me in a slight singsong voice that one might use with a child. *Don't forget, always use flat-leaf Italian parsley—that American parsley has no flavor,* he tells me again and again, each time as if for the first time, as if it were a revelation, a gift for being a good girl. A good girl is quiet and doesn't tell secrets. Maybe it's more comfortable for me to play that role with him. To pretend that I don't know what I know. Simply to watch him cook, with innocence and awe, ignoring the rage that has settled inside me like a too-heavy meal that I can't digest.

My hand is shaky as I hold the camera, and my questions are awkward—*Why do you have to fry the tomato paste first?*—skirting around the deeper questions. I don't compose my shots so much as follow the action, follow behind, like a toddler. This against my father's control and expertise with his own materials: bay leaf, butcher knife, pepper mill. He makes it look so easy and I stumble. The kitchen is where his power is, perhaps the only place where he has any real power.

The Thanksgiving after Gilda and Miriam died, my father wasn't feeling well, so I decided I would make the meal myself, with the help of my husband. My first Thanksgiving dinner, after years of watching my father cook. He was weak and pale, and had lost a lot of weight. I forbade him even to come into the kitchen. We had a small group of family and friends over, and there were candles and appetizers and music and it felt right, that I had finally made a home for myself and could share it in this way. But my father barely spoke to anyone all night. He sat in a chair by the kitchen door and watched helplessly as my husband and I prepared the meal. *Are you sure you want to use that pot?* he would call out, or *You need more salt than that.* Food has been the only way he knows to communicate, to show his love. And it is also a mask that he hides behind, a kind of bravado that disguises his fragile sense of his own worth. He sat and wrung his hands, growing more and more panicked as the cooking went on, more and more removed from the life around him.

At the end of the video, Gilda and Susan set the table. Gilda's good dishes, white with tiny gold stars and gold around the rim. My father is mixing the macaroni with the béchamel and the sauce. Then the mozzarella and the grated pecorino. Mix again. More cheese on top. He puts the huge baking pan into the oven. Enough to feed an army. He leans against the counter, wiping the perspiration from his face. This is work. Suddenly it seems very quiet—the kitchen air is thick with exhaustion and anticipation, mingled with the aroma rising from the oven. I think of questions I should ask, what more information I might need to record, but I'm all out of questions. The shoot feels done, we're done here. Soon my father will take out the baked ziti and present it at the table. We will marvel at its beauty, and then I will sit down with my ghosts and eat.

.   .   .

MIRIAM DIED IN the middle of October 1997. She had been home from the hospital after treatment for her cancer just one day before. At the funeral, my mother and I had sat together in front of the urn with Miriam's ashes, my father sat behind us with my husband. The whole time, my father leaned forward to hold my mother's hand and mine. The hall had been packed with Miriam's friends and colleagues, and even some of the politicians she had worked for during her activist years in Harlem. One by one people stood and gave testimony to her courage and compassion, stories I had never heard about her from long before I was born. The funeral was a celebration of her life, and yet coming home I had cried until it felt like my body had dried up, as if inside me there were a desert where blood, lymph, and salt water once flowed.

When I got back to my apartment that night the phone rang. It was Marie—there were tears in her voice. *Grandma died tonight,* she whispered. Gilda had been ill for a long time, but she had still seemed so strong when I saw her last, a couple of weeks before. But the Alzheimer's had devastated her mind. She kept saying to me, *I want to go home, why won't they let me go home to Harlem?* Marie and I cried together on the phone. She had made all the arrangements for the funeral—for the last few years she had taken care of Gilda almost single-handedly, helping her eat, bathing her, a kind of intimacy Gilda and I had never known. Before she hung up, Marie said, *Grandma loved you.* After Gilda died, Marie and her husband sold the house and moved to a new development in a nearly rural area of Pennsylvania. They have a beautiful home alongside a creek. Early in the mornings, deer come and graze in their backyard.

I spent a year after that lying on my couch, watching endless reruns of old television shows. It was as though I had lost twelve months of my life, or perhaps more accurately, that I had left my body behind and gone to a place for which I have no memory. I know only that I stopped looking in the mirror. For a year, I never once looked into my own eyes. But sometime the following spring, I woke up. I had applied for a grant to make a film in Sicily based on the story of Persephone, and that April, I found out that I got it. Caught in a current of energy I could no longer deny—the electric feeling of being alive again—I bought a ticket and packed my bags. All that was left to do was to renew my passport, which had expired a couple of years before.

But there was a problem with my passport. The paperwork from when my father had changed my name before we moved to New Jersey had been incomplete. He had forgotten to mail in the most important form, and it had lain unsigned, along with some other old papers, in a box in his closet ever since. Somehow the passport had been issued the first time with my new name, but they weren't going to renew it without the proper documentation. So early one morning at the end of April, I went with my mother and my father to family court. We sat in the hot, crowded waiting room for hours, waiting for our case to come up before the judge. My father was ill that day, his skin cold and damp. Every now and then he shivered, then he'd doze off, waking up with a start—*Is it our turn yet?* My mother had bought a stack of fashion and gossip magazines and flipped through them, asking me about the details of my trip and making small talk with my father when he opened his eyes. There they were, together, my parents. My father, unwell but never complaining, shifting around on the hard plastic seat trying to get comfortable as the hours wore on. And my mother, stealing worried glances at my father, getting up to bring him a bottle of water, a damp paper towel for his forehead.

All around us were tired-looking mothers holding babies and watching from the corners of their eyes as their other children ran around the room. Men sat sullenly next to some of the women, reading newspapers and checking their watches. Finally our names were called over the loudspeaker. We went into a large courtroom, where a judge sat high up on his bench, flanked by two American flags. We stood before him, my mother on the left, my father on the right, me in between. I looked at both of them, wondered what the judge thought of our hobbled little family. Could he see that I had my mother's eyes and cheekbones, my father's mouth and small, wiry build? Could he see how their skin blended in me? The hearing was to determine whether my father was actually my biological father, and whether he was contesting his paternity. The judge asked each of my parents if they had had sexual intercourse sometime in 1965. I cringed like a schoolgirl at the thought of them having sex. He asked my mother if she gave birth to me nine months later. When the judge said, *For the record, how old is the child now?* and my mother said, *Thirty-three,* the whole room erupted in laughter: my parents, the judge, the court stenographer, and the armed officers. I laughed, too, at the absurdity of the situation, at how much it took to finally legitimize me. When the judge posed the final question, my father said he wouldn't contest the paternity. *No, I'm her father—just look at us.* And everybody laughed again.

Epilogue

The first place I went in Sicily was Enna, a village in the mountains at the navel of the island where, according to the myth, Persephone was abducted by Hades. The serene, clear lake where she was picking flowers when he first saw and desired her was called Lago Pergusa. I didn't know what form my film would take, but I knew I wanted the story to begin there. I had just a small bag with me, some clothes, a notebook, my Super-8 camera, and a few rolls of film. On the bus to the town, which wound its way around the mountains at a terrifying speed, I asked the driver in my uncertain, childlike Italian how I could get to the lake. He said to me in English, *It's not possible to go there anymore.* It turned out that the lake was now surrounded by a racetrack. We drove by it, and I saw cars buzzing around in a circle, belching black fumes into the sky. I could barely make out the lake in the center—it looked flat and gray, dead as a pool of asphalt.

At the top of the mountain on which Enna clings, there is a large, flat rock, la Rocca di Cerere. It's where Demeter is said to have searched for her daughter when she learned of her theft, her great hawk's eyes scanning across the land for some sign, some trace. The view from there is astounding—the island's body unfolding like a woman's, all curves and undulation as far as the eye can see. The earth itself is variegated, patches of green fields and brown fields, and black fields where the soil has been turned, dark wrinkled outgrowths of rock, and gray snaking roads. It looks like skin, dry in some places, smooth in others, old and young skin, pale and dark skin.

After Enna I made my way to Palermo. I had longed to see this, the ancient chaotic capital of Sicily, the site of thousands of years of invasion and violation, accommodation and amalgamation. It had been claimed by the Greeks, Romans, Phoenicians, Arabs, Normans, Spanish, and French. And still Palermo stood, scarred, enriched, defiant. I spent days walking the city, amazed by the layers of history, exposed as raw nerve, on the surfaces of buildings, in the dark eyes of the people I met. Cathedrals that had once been mosques that had in their turn once been temples of the old gods. The undulating language its own syncretic architecture, formed in the breath and on the tongue. It was the words of Arabic origin that I first recognized as I walked those streets, listening to the conversations of the people I passed. They were words that I had heard in the Bronx and in our house in New Jersey: *zia, zucca, zagara.* My Italian ancestors, those who came from this island and those who came from the mountains of Calabria, were a mingled people, whose disputed bloodlines had found their way to me. In America, the descendants of southern Italian immigrants learned only to see shame in this complex heritage, not beauty, not strength. But when I looked at the faces of the people around me, I saw my father's face, and Gilda's face. And I saw my own.

The last night I was in Palermo, I was invited to a party by a young Sicilian couple I had met in a café. The woman had blond hair in dreadlocks and sea-green eyes; her boyfriend had dark, tightly curled hair like my father's, and his skin was shades browner than mine. The party was in a squat in an old part of town called La Kalsa. It had been Palermo's Arab quarter, and its name retains the memory of Sicily's centuries-long connection to the Arab world. After that, La Kalsa was where the poorest people lived, invisible to the wealthy, who lived in grand houses by the sea, and ignored by city officials, who did little to alleviate the hunger and sickness that plagued the neighborhood. During the Second World War it had been heavily bombed, but never rebuilt. People still lived in the ruins of some of the buildings. The dreadlocked woman said to me, *Palermo is like your Harlem—we are the blacks of Italy. And La Kalsa is the Harlem of Palermo.* Along with the poor and working-class Sicilians, immigrants from Africa and Asia now called the neighborhood their home.

My new Sicilian friends took me for a walk around La Kalsa before the party. From every direction I could smell the sea. Women sat on lawn chairs outside their doors, cutting pieces of fruit for their children. Young men leaned on old, beat-up cars, smoking and listening to the rap music that was coming from one of the apartments above them. Two little Bengali girls with long black braids passed us, walking hand in hand, their matching pink scarves floating in gentle waves behind them. They were speaking to each other in Sicilian.

As we came to where the party was, I saw a woman come out from a doorway. At first glance, she looked like some kind of ghost, her skin was so white. When I looked closely, I saw that she was African; her face was covered with white cake makeup, but around her ears I could see her brown skin. She had on a straight blond wig and a miniskirt that she kept tugging down. Her ankles wobbled in her high-heeled shoes as she walked down the street. I wanted to run after her, try to talk to her. The couple told me that she was a prostitute, that a lot of young African women were. It was the only work they could find. They were closely guarded by their pimps, part of the mafia that ran that particular trade. *They'll hurt you if you ask her too many questions,* they told me. *But why do they hide their faces like that?* I asked them. *To make themselves more beautiful to Sicilian men,* the boyfriend said matter-of-factly, raising his eyebrow as if I had not understood something that would have been obvious to anyone else.

The party was in a building that had been partially blown up during the war. The top two floors had been decimated, the remaining structure left exposed to the sun and the wind. Wild plants grew in the cracks between the walls, feral cats leaned out of the remnants of windows. The two bottom floors were inhabited by families and young people—a group of artists shared the squat, friends of the couple I was with. NWA was playing on the stereo, *Fuck the police!* People were dancing, or making out in corners, or sitting on busted couches, smoking pot and talking over the music. Again, the elemental sounds of Sicilian, low and sonorous, so much like the way Luigi spoke. One of the people who lived there was a young woman from Portugal named Amalia, whose mother was Angolan. Amalia was tall and voluptuous, with coffee-colored skin and a loose Afro that she played with constantly, smoothing it down, fluffing it up, twirling strands of hair absent-mindedly. We spoke most of the night in a mixture of broken Italian and broken English, excited to have found each other, two biracial women from different ends of the African diaspora, each of us with a strong emotional connection to Sicily. Her boyfriend was from La Kalsa— she had met him at a concert in Lisbon. Amalia had been living in Palermo for a few months, but she wasn't sure how long she'd stay because she hadn't found a job.

Because my hotel was so far away, and the neighborhood was

particularly rough after dark, Amalia invited me to stay over. The party had gone on all night—I managed to get just a couple of hours' sleep, curled up on a pallet in her room. In the morning, we went down to the small café around the corner for a cornetto and a cappuccino. There was a large, open field nearby, an incongruous sight in such a resolutely urban space. It had once been a block of apartment buildings and shops—they had been leveled during the war, but their foundations could still be seen just beneath the soil and patches of dry tufts of grass. A group of boys were playing soccer there, running from one side of the field to the other, bouncing the ball off their heads. Some of the boys were African, their skin black as obsidian against the olive and light brown skin of the Sicilians. I left Amalia and sat down in the grass to watch them. The boys shouted and laughed, competed and showed off for each other. The sun grew hot against my shoulders, and a faint breeze rustled the fronds of the palm trees that stood along one side of the field. For a moment I lost track of where I was—was this Palermo, or Cairo, or Lagos, or Harlem?

THERE IS A Sicilian proverb: *Cu bona reda voli fari, di figghia fimmina avi a cumincinari.* One translation is, "A good descent starts with a girl." Descent as heritage, lineage, blood. Sybela and her unnamed mother, Luisa and Gilda, Miriam and my mother, my mother and me: a lineage of mothers and daughters losing each other and finding each other over and over again. All these women who were once girls, perhaps remained girls in the secret, unbroken, untamed places inside them. My heritage, what they have all passed on to me, is the loss, the search, the story.

Descent, of course, also carries a mythic meaning—Persephone's descent into the underworld. This underworld is nothing like our modern vision of hell. It's the realm of the ancestors, the realm of memory. Persephone is transformed from captive girl to queen of the underworld when she eats pomegranate seeds—the seeds, the bleeding fruit, keep her tied to Hades and his kingdom forever. From that time on, she must divide her life between light and dark, winter and spring, mother and lover, innocence and power. In most versions of the myth, Hades forces her to eat the seeds, and Persephone recounts this violation helplessly and tearfully to Demeter. But in Ovid's *Metamorphoses,* Persephone eats the fruit herself, stealing a pomegranate from a tree in Hades' vast, lush garden. She breaks open the rough red skin of the fruit, and puts the seven seeds into her mouth.

I LIKE THIS image of Persephone better, choosing her own fate.